The Clint Eastwood Westerns

The
Clint Eastwood
Westerns

JAMES L. NEIBAUR

ROWMAN & LITTLEFIELD
Lanham • Boulder • New York • London

Published by Rowman & Littlefield
A wholly owned subsidary of The Rowman & Littlefield Publishing Group, Inc.
4501 Forbes Boulevard, Suite 200, Lanham, Maryland 20706
www.rowman.com

Unit A, Whitacre Mews, 26-34 Stannary Street, London SE11 4AB

British Library Cataloguing in Publication Information Available

Library of Congress Cataloging-in-Publication Data
Neibaur, James L., 1958–
  The Clint Eastwood westerns / James L. Neibaur.
    pages cm
  Includes bibliographical references and index.
  ISBN 978-1-4422-4503-7 (hardback : alk. paper) — ISBN 978-1-4422-4504-4 (ebook)
1. Eastwood, Clint, 1930—Criticism and interpretation. 2. Western films—United
States—History and criticism. 3. Western television programs—United States—History
and criticism. I. Title.
  PN2287.E37N45 2015
  791.4302'8092—dc23   2014037382

♾™ The paper used in this publication meets the minimum requirements of American
National Standard for Information Sciences—Permanence of Paper for Printed Library
Materials, ANSI/NISO Z39.48-1992.

Printed in the United States of America

To my son, Max.
I am so proud of all that you have become.

Contents

Acknowledgments

For proofing, rewrite suggestions, interviews, inspiration, support, and encouragement, I thank Terri Lynch, Katie Carter, Ted Post, Jordan Young, Pamelyn Ferdin, Scott Rivers, Ted Okuda, Scott McGee, Scott Spiegel, Tammy Locke, Billy Curtis, Roger Ebert, Eli Wallach, Patti Miller, and Dave Kehr.

Introduction

Clint Eastwood has now been established as an icon of western cinema, and this is not only due to his keen filmmaking savvy. Along with becoming one of the finest directors of his time, he has also completely redefined the parameters of the western movie hero. Once Eastwood's "Man with No Name" rode onto the scene in Sergio Leone's landmark Italian film *A Fistful of Dollars* (1964), the idea of western heroism was completely revamped for modern and more progressive audiences. The new hero was darker, more cynical, and more dangerous than his predecessors.

The western genre has always been a quintessential staple of pop culture's history. Pulp western novels were popular centuries ago, usually based on the actual exploits of real-life gunslingers and lawmen. In films, the western genre dates back as early as narrative cinema. Edwin S. Porter's landmark one-reel silent *The Great Train Robbery* (1903) was among the very first films that used editing to tell a story. This story about the robbing of a railroad car, with bandits being pursued on horseback by the law, became so popular, existing reports say, that audiences insisted the ten-minute film be run again and again. Porter used cross-cut editing techniques to enhance the action, with a shot of the pursuing lawmen then cutting to a shot of the fleeing bandits. Over 100 years old, the film remains one of the core examples of the western movie structure.

Throughout the growth and refinement of the filmmaking process, western movies continued to proliferate, experiencing periods where they were produced by the dozens every year. In the silent era, the western hero came in many guises, from the stoicism of William S. Hart, to the daredevil antics of Tom Mix. Westerns soon became the domain of actors like John Wayne and Randolph Scott, who specialized in the genre, as well as actors like James Stewart and Gary Cooper, who appeared in western films on a regular basis. Directors like Howard Hawks, John Ford, Budd Boetticher, Delmer Daves, Burt Kennedy, and Anthony Mann all contributed excellent films to the western genre. Ford, especially, explored deeper themes in such films as *She Wore a Yellow Ribbon* (1949), *The Searchers* (1956), and *The Man Who Shot Liberty Valance* (1962), all of which featured John Wayne. Wayne also starred in Howard Hawks's top westerns *Red River* (1948) and *Rio Bravo* (1959), making him the quintessential star of the genre, and the only one other than Clint Eastwood to reach true iconic status.

Saturday matinees from the 1920s through the 1940s were filled with the B-level antics of cowboy favorites like Roy Rogers, Gene Autry, and William "Hopalong Cassidy" Boyd. In the 1950s, westerns enjoyed massive popularity on television, which offered everything from the action of *The Cisco Kid* and *The Lone Ranger* to the more serious, adult-oriented *Gunsmoke*, *Wagon Train*, and *Bonanza*. As the 1950s ended, television was featuring more serious westerns along the lines of films like John Ford's *Wagon Master* (1950) and Fred Zinnemann's *High Noon* (1952); these westerns concentrated on stories and characters. *Gunsmoke* is probably the best example; the immensely popular television western lasted twenty years on television after having been on radio from 1952 to 1961.

Rawhide, a TV series depicting the trials and tribulations of a cattle drive, premiered in January 1959. It starred Eric Fleming and Clint Eastwood, who were, at the time, actors of little note. Eastwood had been a contract player at Universal Studios and had made a few films for RKO, but he had not yet made much of an impact. This series, on which he played Rowdy Yates, was very popular and made Clint Eastwood's name well known. As an actor, however, Eastwood did not like being locked into a TV series and limited to playing one character, so he looked into the possibility of directing some episodes. The producers didn't want to take a chance on him directing, so they allowed him the freedom to make guest appearances on other shows, and to also appear in movies if they were shot during *Rawhide*'s summer hiatus.

Italian filmmaker Sergio Leone was a passionate fan of the American western film, but his vision was much different. His vision was to extend beyond the conventional "code of the west" that appeared in western movies and TV shows and make films where that code was completely jettisoned. His western hero was not above shooting an adversary in the back, or seeking vengeance with no regard to the law. Leone wanted a film that was graphically violent and filled with action, but also brilliantly acted with a sound narrative structure. When he saw Clint Eastwood in an episode of the American television show *Rawhide*, he cast the actor as the central figure in *A Fistful of Dollars* (1964).

Clint Eastwood made three films for Leone (casually known as the Dollars trilogy), and his career became more established. Continuing to explore western cinema, as well as other genres, Eastwood had risen from a bit player, to a supporting TV star, to one of the most gifted actors and filmmakers in American cinema, finally reaching iconic status.

While this book concentrates on analyzing the western films that Eastwood made for Leone, Don Siegel, and with himself as director, there are bracketing chapters that discuss his non-westerns like *Play Misty for Me* (1971), *Dirty Harry* (1971), *Escape from Alcatraz* (1979), and other important movies that helped inform his consistent work in the western genre. Each western film will be carefully assessed as to its importance to the genre, to cinema, and to Eastwood's own career.

And while most studies believe that Clint Eastwood made only ten western films, this book extends to include *Coogan's Bluff* (1968), *The Beguiled* (1971), *Paint Your Wagon* (1969), and *Bronco Billy* (1980), all of which are uncharacteristic westerns, either for being a musical, set in modern times, or set in the south, for example. Eastwood investigated aspects of the western format in each of these films, and while they may not be traditionally placed in the western genre, there are elements of the western within their context to include them here.

CHAPTER 1

Early Life, First Films, and TV Success

Clinton Eastwood Jr. was born May 30, 1930, in San Francisco, California, the son of Ruth (née Runner; January 18, 1909–February 4, 2006), an IBM factory worker, and Clinton Eastwood Sr. (June 11, 1906–July 21, 1970), a steelworker and migrant worker. Weighing a whopping eleven-and-a-half pounds at birth, he was nicknamed "Samson" by attending nurses. Eastwood has a sister, Jeanne, born in 1934.

Eastwood attended Oakland (California) Technical High School, where his tall stature and easy manner attracted the drama teachers, but he refused their requests to try out for school plays. He worked several jobs during this period of his life, from gold caddy to firefighter, before being drafted, in 1951, by the U.S. Army and stationed at Fort Ord, California. Eastwood married Maggie Johnson in 1953.

While stationed at Ord, Eastwood was nearby when a Universal Studios film crew was shooting portions of a movie location. The imposing six-foot-four-inch soldier was noticed by the film crew as he had been by his high school drama teachers. Eastwood was approached by a man named Chuck Hill, who later snuck him into Universal Studios and introduced him to cameraman Irving Glassberg. Glassberg arranged for Eastwood to perform a screen test for director Arthur Lubin. Lubin liked Eastwood's look and his manner, but realized his acting was very stiff and amateurish. Lubin recommended the newcomer attend a few acting classes to at least learn the rudiments of the craft, and a contract was arranged in 1954. Eastwood's pay was initially $100 per week.

While under contract at Universal, Clint Eastwood was put in several films, often in small, uncredited parts. In 1955 he appeared as a lab technician in *Revenge of the Creature*, and also acted in the sci-fi film *Tarantula* and the Francis the Talking Mule comedy *Francis in the Navy*. Eastwood's lack of experience is

1

Eastwood during his early years as an actor.

evident in these early roles, where he invariably plays an amiable dumb ox or a character on the periphery that barely registers.

His contract at Universal was not renewed, so Eastwood went over to RKO studios to appear in films like *The First Traveling Saleslady* (1956) and *Escapade in Japan* (1957). In 1958 Eastwood appeared in a couple of western films, including *Ambush at Cimarron Pass*, which he continues to call the worst western ever made.

In 1959 Eastwood was hired to co-star with young actor Eric Fleming for a new western TV series called *Rawhide*. Since Eastwood was at the point in his career where a second job digging ditches for swimming pools was paying more than acting, he agreed to do the series. However, he was not quite prepared for the level of popularity television would offer once *Rawhide* premiered on January 9, 1959. Eastwood was quickly elevated to household-name status as Rowdy Yates, a member of a cattle drive in the 1860s. *Rawhide* became the fifth longest running western series on television, lasting from 1959 to 1966. After a series of small, insignificant parts, Clint Eastwood now had steady work and recognition as an actor. But he wasn't satisfied.

Rawhide

When Clint Eastwood began shooting the first *Rawhide* TV episodes in 1958, television was inundated with western series. *Wyatt Earp, Broken Arrow, Have Gun Will Travel, Maverick, Wagon Train, The Rifleman, Bat Masterson, Wanted Dead or Alive,* and *Gunsmoke* were all flourishing. TV westerns had gotten away from series like *The Lone Ranger* and *The Cisco Kid,* wanting to instead have deeper stories that would appeal more to adults. It would seem that with the market so saturated with westerns, another one would not likely stand out.

Rawhide was created by Charles Marquis Warren, a writer-director with a background in western films and TV. The gist of each show featured Rowdy Yates (Clint Eastwood) and Gil Favor (Eric Fleming) heading a cattle drive and coming across people along the trail, and getting involved in whatever dramatic events were going on in their lives. *Rawhide* achieved viewership early on as each episode would invariably feature a noted star as a guest, and the plot would revolve around him or her. Advertising recognizable guest stars with solid movie credits allowed the program to stand out among the many other westerns. Plus, the catchy theme song ("rollin', rollin', rollin'") penned by Dimitri Tiomkin and Ned Washington, and sung by Frankie Laine, became an unlikely chart hit.

In order to keep the viewership that *Rawhide* initially attracted, Charles Marquis Warren and the other producers realized the aesthetics of the show must be good, so they concentrated on getting solid stories from top writers and hired successful directors like Richard Whorf, Andrew McLaglen, and Ted Post. Post recalled in an interview with the author:

> Warren directed a few of the first season episodes himself. Very slow, very rigid. Clint told me he didn't like working with him. I would give the actors some freedom, ask them for their input into the character or scene. Warren would dictate. Actors don't like to work that way.

Rawhide was also courageous enough to explore more controversial issues. There are episodes that deal with drug addiction, racism, alternative religious practices, and the macabre.

Eastwood was pleased with the steady work and regular paycheck, but felt limited by his portrayal. Rowdy Yates was not a forceful, charismatic character, but a rather callow follower. According to Ted Post:

> Clint used to say he and Eric Fleming were co-stars, but "I was the stupid one." Fleming was difficult. He didn't like Charles Warren, and wasn't too crazy about me because I saw that he was a big ham.

Eastwood as Rowdy Yates on TV's *Rawhide*.

Clint worked hard to do a good job, but Fleming was always threatening to quit the show if he didn't get his way.

Despite these misgivings, Eastwood managed to get along with Fleming and was impressed with the actor's ability to easily memorize a page of dialogue after one reading. Rowdy Yates was really more meant to be the supporting character, and Fleming's was the lead. Of course, looking back on the show in hindsight, Rowdy Yates is the more noticeable one because of the fame Eastwood gained later on. Shooting *Rawhide* was quite grueling. Eastwood would film the show six days a week usually working twelve-hour days. During the show's first season, Eastwood earned $750 per episode.

One of the advantages of working on a hit series that used noted actors as guest stars was to observe the working methods of veteran performers. Among those who guested on *Rawhide* during its run include Nick Adams, Claude Akins, Eddie Albert, Mary Astor, Frankie Avalon, James Best, Charles Bronson, Lon Chaney Jr., James Coburn, Robert Culp, Brian Donlevy, Dan Duryea, Buddy Ebsen, Barbara Eden, Jack Elam, Anne Francis, Alan Hale Jr., Dwayne Hickman, Earl Holliman, Sherry Jackson, Brian Keith, George Kennedy, Martin Landau, Suzanne Lloyd, June Lockhart, Jack Lord, Peter Lorre, Jock Mahoney, Darren McGavin, Burgess Meredith, Vera Miles, Martin Milner, Elizabeth Montgomery, Agnes Moorehead, Leslie Nielsen, Leonard Nimoy, Warren Oates, Susan Oliver, Debra Paget, Luana Patten, Edward Platt, Cesar Romero, Marion Ross, William Schallert, Harry Dean Stanton, Barbara Stanwyck, Bob Steele, Woody Strode, Barbara Stuart, Lee Van Cleef, Chill Wills, Marie Windsor, Ed Wynn, and Dick York.

The November 1961 *Rawhide* episode titled "Incident of the Black Sheep" has a special significance as being the one viewed by Sergio Leone to assess Clint Eastwood's possibility to play the central character in *A Fistful of Dollars*. In this episode, Rowdy Yates rides into a nearby town when a sheepherder gets injured on the cattle drive and needs medical attention. Confronting prejudice, getting in a bar fight, and being sent to jail are among the things Yates experiences in this episode. His performance was enough for Leone to cast him. The structure of this episode is also a bit similar to *A Fistful of Dollars*, being that they're both about strangers riding into a town and then getting involved with its residents.

Clint Eastwood was by no means Leone's first choice. Henry Fonda, Charles Bronson, James Coburn, Rory Calhoun, and Henry Silva were all considered. The stars showed little interest in appearing in a low budget film in Italy. Italian films at this time were usually the sword-and-sandal Hercules efforts that played to limited audiences in the United States. While Italy did indeed boast the talents of such fine filmmakers as Roberto Rossellini, Vittorio De Sica, and Federico Fellini, most of what was produced in their mainstream was dismissible.

The film was to have a $200,000 budget, with the lead actor receiving $15,000. This would not be considered a particularly strong career move for any established American actor, but Eastwood was willing to consider taking a chance. He longed to extend past the tedium of playing the same role week after week. After his interest in directing a few episodes was thwarted, he took the opportunity to make guest appearances on other shows, and wanted to exercise the freedom he had to do movies during the show's hiatus. (On an episode of *Mr. Ed*, created by old friend Arthur Lubin, for example, Eastwood was cast as himself. Such was his stardom as a result of *Rawhide*.)

Leone and his fellow producers from Germany and Spain contacted the William Morris Agency, who represented Clint Eastwood. They inquired as to his availability to star in a film they planned to produce in Italy titled *El Magnifico Strangero* (*The Magnificent Stranger*). At first he was not interested, believing quite logically that a western made in Europe would be an artistic and financial disaster. His agency, however, had promised the producers that he would at least look at the script.

Eastwood read through the very thick script for *The Magnificent Stranger* and recognized the story was lifted from Akira Kurosawa's Japanese samurai movie *Yojimbo* (1961). Eastwood was an admirer of Kurosawa, and of this film, and was intrigued by the creative idea of transforming it into a western drama. The actor was also smart enough to be aware that Kurosawa's work was inspired by his love of American western films.

By the 1960s, western movies had been eclipsed by the plethora of westerns on television. Audiences were more than satisfied with the western adventures they could see for free in the comfort of their homes. Even the best westerns, however, employed consistent conventions that had never been challenged. Eastwood recognized the intention of the *Magnificent Stranger* screenplay was to make such a challenge, with the story, the structure, and the central character. Eastwood had his wife read through the script, and she was also impressed with its very different perspective. Having no work lined up during the months that *Rawhide* was on hiatus, Eastwood accepted the role.

CHAPTER 2

A Fistful of Dollars (1964)

(Constantin Film Produktion, Jolly Film, Ocean Films; distributed in the United States by United Artists)

Original Title: *Per un pugno di dollari*

Director: Sergio Leone

Screenplay: Víctor Andrés Catena, Jaime Comas Gil, Sergio Leone; story by Adriano Bolzoni, Víctor Andrés Catena, Sergio Leone

Producers: Arrigo Colombo, Giorgio Papi

Assistant Producer: Piero Santini

Music: Ennio Morricone

Cinematography: Massimo Dallamano, Federico G. Larraya

Editing: Roberto Cinquini, Alfonso Santacana

Cast: Clint Eastwood (Joe); Marianne Koch (Marisol); Gian Maria Volonté (Ramón Rojo); Wolfgang Lukschy (John Baxter); Sieghardt Rupp (Esteban Rojo); Joseph Egger (Piripero); Antonio Prieto (Don Miguel Benito Rojo); José Calvo (Silvanito); Margarita Lozano (Consuelo Baxter); Daniel Martín (Julián); Benito Stefanelli (Rubio); Mario Brega (Chico); Bruno Carotenuto (Antonio Baxter); Aldo Sambrell (Rojo Gang Member); Raf Baldassarre (Juan De Dios); Antonio Moreno (Juan de dios); Nino Del Arco (Jesus); Juan Cortés (Cavalry Captain); José Riesgo (Mexican Cavalry Captain); Nosher Powell (Cowboy); Enrique Santiago (Fausto); Umberto Spadaro (Miguel); Fernando Sánchez Polack (Rojo Gang Member Crushed by Wine Cask); José Canalejas, Álvaro de Luna, Antonio Pica, Nazzareno Natale, Jose Halufi (Rojo Gang Members); Lorenzo Robledo, Luis Barboo, Julio Pérez Tabernero (Baxter Gunmen); Frank Braña, Antonio Molino Rojo, William R. Thompkins (Baxter Gang Members); Edmondo Tieghi (Mexican Soldier); Lee Miller (Man at Bar).

Voice Dubs: Dubbing actor (followed by screen actor in parentheses): Oreste Lionello (Raf Baldassarre), Anna Miserocchi (Margarita Lozano), Luigi Pavese (José Calvo), Nino Pavese (Daniel Martin), Bruno Persa (Sieghardt

Rupp), Mario Pisu (Antonio Prieto), Enrico Maria Salerno (Clint East-
wood), Rita Savagnone (Marianne Koch), Renato Turi (Mario Brega).
Budget: $200,000 (estimated)
Gross: $14,500,000 (USA)
Release Dates: Italy (September 12, 1964); USA (January 18, 1967)
Running Time: 99 minutes
Sound Mix: Mono (Western Electric Sound System)
Color: Technicolor
Aspect Ratio: 2.35: 1
Availability: DVD (Fox Searchlight); Blu-ray (Fox Searchlight)

A Fistful of Dollars may not be the first western produced in Italy, but its success and subsequent impact has resulted in it being known as the first "spaghetti western." The style utilized in this film challenged the conventions of the American western and helped redefine them for a new generation. *A Fistful of Dollars* is also significant for Eastwood's stoic performance. Reaching well past the parameters of TV character Rowdy Yates or any of the amiable supporting players he'd essayed in past films, Eastwood here commands every scene in which he appears, and does so with an economy of movement.

At the time this film was made, the conventions used in American western movies seemed a bit quaint and dated. Not that the western film was no longer an active genre: the first half of the 1960s boasted such significant western productions as *The Magnificent Seven* (1960), *Ride the High Country* (1961), and *Lonely Are the Brave* (1962). However, too often the American western displayed the sort of ordinary fare that was sometimes met with derision in Italy for the stock conventions contained within the narrative and filmmaking. Leone's vision was to take the rudiments of the Japanese samurai film, combine it with the cinematic language of Italian filmmaking, and transfer these to a western setting. The most significant Italian cinema had been the neorealist period that gave us movies like *Rome: Open City* (*Roma città aperta*, 1945), *Paisan* (1946), *Shoeshine* (*Sciuscia*, 1947), and *The Bicycle Thief* (*Bicycle Thieves*, *Ladri di biciclette*, 1948) from directors like Roberto Rossellini and Vittorio De Sica. These films represented changes in the collective psyche of the Italian people, examining such states as poverty, injustice, and desperation. Leone wanted that sort of base realism within the context of a western movie.

As stated in the previous chapter, Clint Eastwood was not Leone's first choice to play the title role in his script titled *El magnifico strangero* (*The Magnificent Stranger*). Leone wanted to defy convention with the casting and feature Henry Fonda in the role. Fonda, known for playing affable, heroic types, would be working completely against type as the looming, cynical presence that was the stranger. Fonda, a Hollywood veteran who was still commanding starring performances in movies, proved to be too expensive for the low budget production. Leone also considered using older western actor Rory Calhoun in the part, but he turned it down. Charles Bronson turned it down because he didn't like the script. Eastwood recalled for Damon Wise in the *Independent*:

> I got the part because I was cheap. Sergio spoke very little English, and I didn't speak any Italian at that time. So we got together with an interpreter when I reached Rome. And through the interpreter—plus a lot of hand signals—we kind of got the idea.

The plot of *A Fistful of Dollars* features a drifter[1] (Clint Eastwood) who rides quietly and ominously into a Mexican village on the United States border. The stranger notices that this town of San Miguel is dominated by a conflict between two gangster lords: John Baxter (W. Lukschy) and Ramón Rojo (Gian Maria Volonté). The stranger is confronted by four men in the Baxters' gang and kills them in an unflinching, efficient manner. He is then hired by Ramón's brother Esteban Rojo (S. Rupp) to join their gang. Considering himself separate from either faction, but giving the appearance that he supports both, the stranger figures out a way to play one side against the other.

When Clint Eastwood first read the script, he recognized it as having been inspired by Akira Kurosawa's Japanese samurai film *Yojimbo* (1961). Eastwood told Roger Ebert in a 2002 interview:

> I didn't know if you could make the jump to the big screen. A few people had. Steve McQueen did small roles and built himself up as a name in pictures. But when I came out of the foreign thing, it was strictly a luck deal, a rolling of the dice. "Fistful" cost about $200,000 to make. It was a Western shot in Spain as an Italian-German-Spanish coproduction, with a screenplay based on a Japanese samurai movie. All the producers were arguing among themselves about who was going to pay the bills. It could have been an absolute disaster. But, we got lucky with it. And it turned out Sergio Leone was for real. We both came out of the box together.

However, when Clint Eastwood arrived at the location site, he found that the Italian filmmakers knew little about the American west. For instance, Eastwood recalled that the costumes featured a lot of coonskin caps, which were popular with frontier trappers during the Davy Crockett era of the 1820s, but would not have been worn by gunfighters in Mexico some fifty years later, when *A Fistful of Dollars* was set.

As this was a low budget production, Eastwood's creative input was welcome. He even had the freedom to create his own costume, purchasing the black

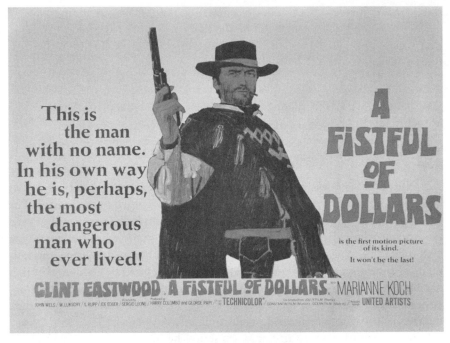

Poster for *A Fistful of Dollars.*

jeans from a sports shop in California, the hat from a wardrobe supplier, the poncho in Spain, and wearing the boots he'd been wearing on *Rawhide*. The cigars that became the character's trademark were purchased from a tobacco store in Beverly Hills. Eastwood cut them into three pieces in order to present the effect of a smaller cigar or cigarello. The actor himself was actually a nonsmoker. Eastwood recalled for Damon Wise:

> I had no idea they'd taste so vile! But I brought those along with me and I gave them to props and we cut them all up. They were long cigars, called Virginia. I made a slew of them that I carried around in my pocket: different lengths to match up with different scenes.

The difference between this film and the Hollywood western was immediate, as explained by Edward Gallafent in *Clint Eastwood: Filmmaker and Star*:

> [T]his Mexico is not what Hollywood uses for Mexico (Southern California or Mexico itself), but somewhere else (actually Almeria, a province of Spain that would presumably have meant little or nothing to many Americans). The effect of this is to accentuate the

remoteness of this film's Mexico, to put it in a different relationship to the United States from that found in the Hollywood western.

The character is defined upon the very first scene when he rides into town on a mule. Leone originally shoots him from the back. As he dismounts to get some water from a well, he sees a child running, crying, and being shot at by bandits who later pummel his father. He also sees a woman who appears to be trapped in a building. This activity is set in the middle of bleak desert surroundings. As the stranger examines the scene, he squints in a very stern, judgmental manner, smiling thinly at the woman who does not return his attention. As Clint Eastwood's only truly noted characterization at the time was the affable Rowdy Yates on television, this expression, and this character's entire manner, was a complete reversal.

Eastwood told author Howard Hughes in his book *Aim for the Heart: The Films of Clint Eastwood*:

> In *Rawhide* I did get awfully tired of playing the conventional white hat. The hero who kisses old ladies and dogs and was kind to everybody. I decided it was time to be an anti-hero.

And in the book *Clint: The Life and Legend*, author Patrick McGilligan stated:

> Eastwood was instrumental in creating the Man with No Name character's distinctive visual style and, although a non-smoker, Leone insisted Eastwood smoke cigars as an essential ingredient of the "mask" he was attempting to create for the loner character.

It is obvious that Clint Eastwood had a firm idea as to how to explore the character in Leone's movie. Rowdy Yates is very good-natured and polite, and nothing about the way Eastwood looks or talks really fits that personality. While he was effective and popular in the *Rawhide* role, his acting strengths lie in another direction.

When the stranger is accosted by four men, who shoot at him and frighten his mule, he ducks into a cantina and befriends the proprietor, Silvanito (José Calvo), who tells him about the feud between the two families who are vying to gain control of the town. After first telling an undertaker to "get three coffins ready," the stranger quietly leaves the inn and confronts the four men who had accosted him earlier. He patiently informs them that while he understands they were having a bit of fun at his expense, his mule does not. He wants an apology for the mule. As one of the men prepares to draw, the stranger pulls out a hand gun and, fanning the hammer, effectively kills the four men. As he passes the undertaker again, he apologizes and says, "four coffins." As evident by this first scene, the standoffs in *A Fistful of Dollars* are very drawn out. A lot of time is spent just switching between close-ups of each gunfighter's face. Leone concentrates on his characters in this manner, rather than simply on the actions of each character.

The stranger is established as one who can kill in cold blood with efficiency and no remorse. He is a cold cynic and a calculating one. He realizes the opportunity to make money when a shipment of gold passes through the town. The gold is said to be en route to a troop of American soldiers in exchange for weapons. The stranger follows the Mexican troops out of town and sees them all killed by members of the Rojo gang, who are dressed in American uniforms. Ramón Rojo is introduced as the biggest badman by his steely eyed expressions as he mows down Mexican soldiers with a machine gun. The Rojos steal the gold.

The stranger takes two of the bodies to a cemetery, ostensibly to bury them. He informs members of both families that two Mexican soldiers survived the attack. The Baxters then hurry to the cemetery to convince the survivors to testify against the Rojos, while the Rojos rush there to kill the survivors. The rivals become engaged in a gunfight, and the stranger uses their being distracted to his advantage. He searches the hacienda for the stolen gold with the intention of taking it for himself. Surprised by the sudden appearance of Ramón's prisoner, Marisol (Marianne Koch), the stranger brings her to the Baxter family, who arrange to trade with the Rojos for their kidnapped son.

There are several distinct antihero elements here. First, unlike the conventional lone cowboy, the stranger does not pick a side and help them. He pits both sides against each other for his own personal gain. His plan to steal from the Rojos is thwarted when the woman discovers him. But even though she is being kept against her will, the stranger does not rescue her. He uses her to incur favor with the Baxter family, continuing to favor both sides so that their elimination of each other might net him a profit. He only changes his mind when he learns more about her plight. Silvanito tells the stranger that Marisol is being held by Ramón as a mistress because he believes her husband cheated him at cards (although he did not).

Leone's filming of the gun battle is a good example of how his style is informed by his love of opera. There is an operatic grace to Leone's presentation, showing a close-up of each gunman's face, centering mostly on his eyes, then cutting away to the person being shot falling over dead. It maintains a rhythm and a pace but also allows us to see the menace of the killer and to dismiss the killed with anonymity, switching to a less intimate medium shot to show them fall to the ground dead. Leone also films from over the shoulder of the shooter to effectively show his vantage point. This was a very new and different way of filming a gunfight at the time. Rather than cutting from one person shooting a gun straight to the victim falling over dead, there are many times when Leone allows the viewer to actually see the bullet hitting the victim, from the perspective of the shooter. This effect came off as far more realistically brutal than what had been found in Hollywood westerns up to that time.

During the trade between the groups, when Marisol's son runs to her, followed by her husband, the Rojos attempt to shoot the husband, and Silvanito tries to stop them. They prepare to kill Silvanito, but he is rescued by the stranger. Nobody wants to engage in a gun battle with the stranger, as he already proved himself to be too fast. He tells Marisol to return to Ramón Rojo and instructs the husband to take the child home. That night, while the Rojos are preoccupied, the stranger frees Marisol, killing the guards and destroying the house so it looks like an attack by the Baxters. The stranger instructs Marisol, her husband, and their son to leave town, giving them some money. When asked by Marisol, "Why do you do this for us?," the stranger replies, "I knew someone like you once. There was no one there to help."

This scene and the stranger's relationship with Marisol are quite important to the film. Without this redeeming quality, it might have been somewhat difficult for audiences to accept the stranger even as an antihero. This way, he is given a quality that makes him a bit likeable, while enough information is still withheld to maintain an aura of mystery. However, this redeeming quality of the stranger remains couched in his cynicism, as he realizes their safety can only be maintained if he thwarts any attempt to find them. The stranger is captured and beaten by the Rojos but retains his stoicism and strength of character. He manages to escape with the help of Piripero (Joseph Egger) who smuggles him in a coffin out of town, which allows him to convalesce in a cave. The Rojos believe the stranger is being hidden in the cantina, so they beat the proprietor, Silvanito. Once Piripero informs the stranger that Silvanito has been beaten, the stranger places a steel plate over his chest inside his shirt, and returns to town to confront Ramón Rojo. Goading him to "aim for the heart," a frustrated Ramón empties his gun firing at the chest of the stranger, as the bullets bounce off the hidden steel plate. The stranger shoots away Ramón's rifle and, fanning the hammer of his pistol, empties his gun, killing all of Ramón's men. The stranger challenges Ramón to fill his rifle before he can load his own pistol. He kills Ramón, while Silvanito kills the unseen Esteban Rojo who is prepared to fire on the stranger from a building. The film ends with the stranger leaving town in the grandest of western movie traditions.

As it challenges the western cinema's conventions, and is inspired by a Japanese samurai film (which itself was inspired by Dashiell Hammett's 1929 book *Red Harvest*), there remains an element of convention in Leone's narrative. Eastwood's character rides into town as a stranger, cleans up the corruption, saves the townsfolk, bids his farewell, and rides out of town. This is certainly a classic structure for a western. It is the filmmaker's presentation of heightened violence and the lead actor's approach to the central character that separate it from the ordinary. Edward Gallafent stated in *Clint Eastwood: Actor and Director*:

> A figure with no past or future related to the town, he is envisioned for a moment as a gothic avenger from some other plane of being, a subject which Eastwood will go on to exploit, in different ways, in *High Plains Drifter* and in *Pale Rider* which has its relevance even to *Unforgiven*.

Along with the heightened violence and the unconventional manner of the central character, Ennio Morricone's score enhanced each scene. Rather than the sweeping orchestral backgrounds of most American westerns (including *The Magnificent Seven* [1960], which also had Japanese samurai source material), the scenes in this film were backed by a smaller, tighter, and more distinctive sound. Instead of instruments from a full orchestra, Morricone utilized such offbeat sounds as gunshots, cracking whips, whistles, chanting voices, and a Fender electric guitar. Although they had known each other since third grade, *A Fistful of Dollars* was Morricone's and Leone's first collaboration. The composer would subsequently work on all of Leone's movies.

Often low budget shoots can be quite grueling, but Eastwood's background in the rushed production of weekly series television prepared him for nearly anything that could happen on the set of this movie. Eastwood recalled for Damon Wise in the *Independent*:

> Leone loved food. He loved food. The first day we filmed, we were shooting in a studio outside of Rome, and we sat down for lunch. We had this huge meal. Spaghetti. I love spaghetti, so I loaded myself up. And then they served wine. Everybody was having wine. So I said, "Okay, I'll have a few glasses of wine, too." Well, we went back to work, and suddenly I realized, "I'm not going to be able to do this." For that first hour or two after lunch everything was pretty much done in slow motion!

Upon completion of this feature, Eastwood returned to America and went back to work on *Rawhide*, satisfied with his work on the film but not expecting it to make much of an impact. He didn't even think it would play in the United States. He was surprised by the film's immediate success in Europe (it was the most successful Italian film in Italy up to that time). Eastwood was initially unable to appreciate the publicity for the film in the trades, because the title had been changed from *The Magnificent Stranger* to *A Fistful of Dollars* only days before its world premiere. Eastwood told the *Independent*:

> I started reading in *Variety* about this picture that was causing quite a stir in Rome and Naples. It was called *Per un pugno di dollari* (*For*

a Fistful of Dollars) and it didn't seem at all familiar to me! I just kept reading about how well this picture was doing. And then, finally, I guess after a couple of weeks of reading about this film, I noticed they said, *A Fistful of Dollars*, starring Clint Eastwood . . ." I thought, "Oh my God, it's that picture!" I didn't know what had happened to it! It didn't even have Sergio Leone's name on it, because he'd changed his credit to Bob Robertson, because he wanted to have an English or American-sounding name. So I didn't get the association until they called me up and asked me to do a second picture.

The film was generating great popularity in Europe but was not released in the United States. In fact, its North American premiere was in Canada in 1966, a full two years after its European release. Eastwood was asked by producers to come out and film another western for Leone in Italy. Eastwood stated that he would like to screen the first film before committing to a second. An Italian print, without subtitles, was sent, and Eastwood screened it for himself and some studio executives. He expected little and played it down for his select audience, but, despite the language barrier, they could all see that a very good film had been produced. Eastwood got back to Leone and agreed to come out and film another western with him. Because of the diversity of languages spoken in the film, *A Fistful of Dollars* was shot silent, with dialogue looped in later. Eastwood did not add his own voice to the soundtrack until the film was released in the United States in 1967.

Despite its having something in common with American western films like *My Darling Clementine* (1946) and *Shane* (1953), *A Fistful of Dollars* is most often compared to *Yojimbo*. Akira Kurosawa certainly noticed a resemblance and sued in court. Leone chose to settle out of court, allowing Kurosawa 15 percent of the film's profits and exclusive distribution rights for Japan, Taiwan, and South Korea. Kurosawa later recalled that he made more money from his percentage of *A Fistful of Dollars* than he did from *Yojimbo*.

When the film finally opened in the United States in early 1967, Clint Eastwood had completed his run on *Rawhide*, had completed two more films for Leone, and had created his own production company. Bosley Crowther of the *New York Times* stated in his review:

> Clearly, the magnet of this picture, which has been a phenomenal success in Italy and other parts of Europe, is this cool-cat bandit who is played by Clint Eastwood, an American cowboy actor who used to do the role of Rowdy in the *Rawhide* series on TV. Wearing a Mexican poncho, gnawing a stub of cheroot and peering intently from under a slouch hat pulled low over his eyes, he is simply another fabrication of a personality, half cowboy and half gangster, going through the ritualistic postures and exercises of each. His distinction is that he succeeds in being ruthless without seeming cruel, fascinating

without being realistic. The other distinction of the picture is that it is full of spectacular violence. Sergio Leone, who directed from a script which we understand is a rewrite of the script of *Yojimbo*, a Japanese samurai picture made by Akira Kurosawa with Toshiro Mifune, has crowded it with such juicy splashes as a big fat fellow being squashed by a rolling barrel, a whole squad of soldiers being massacred, and punctured men spitting gore. Ultimately, the cool, non-hero is beaten to a bloody, swollen pulp, from which he miraculously recovers to go forth and kill his tormentors. Filmed in hard, somber color and paced to a musical score that betrays tricks and themes that sound derivative, *A Fistful of Dollars* is a Western that its sanguine distributors suggest may be loosing a new non-hero on us.

However, not all critics were impressed. Philip French of the *Observer* stated:

> The calculated sadism of the film would be offensive were it not for the neutralising laughter aroused by the ludicrousness of the whole exercise. If one didn't know the actual provenance of the film, one would guess that it was a private movie made by a group of rich European Western fans at a dude ranch. And that their American guest was left to supply his own dialogue from familiar clichés of the genre while they stuck to talking about the plot. Somebody actually says, in the film's sole endearing moment, "It's like playing cowboys and Indians." *A Fistful of Dollars* looks awful, has a flat dead soundtrack, and is totally devoid of human feeling.

Despite critics like French who were taken aback by its progressive approach, audiences, especially younger people, embraced the film. It grossed $4.5 million in its first year, eventually earning $14.5 million at the box office.

A Fistful of Dollars did not make its U.S. network television debut until February 1975. Curiously, for television there was the addition of a new prologue, directed by Monty Hellman and featuring Harry Dean Stanton as a lawman who gives the order for Joe to rid San Miguel of its gangs in return for a pardon. A double and stock footage of Eastwood were used.[2] This prologue was filmed for the sole purpose of giving moral justification for the stranger's pitting the two gangs against each other—and almost entirely changes the stranger's character in the process.

The film ignited a trilogy that made Clint Eastwood a worldwide star. It allowed Sergio Leone to emerge as a director of style and vision. It breathed new life into a dying film genre with a more progressive presentation. And it has withstood the test of time. The Spaghetti Western Database states:

> *A Fistful of Dollars* deserves its place in cinema history. The combined genius of Leone's comic book art visuals and Morricone's piercingly

emotive sounds set a lasting standard that has been rarely matched. The film perhaps lacks some of the depth that the following Leone masterpieces attained, but on the other hand it can boast a tightness of pace that Leone eventually lost sight of as he strove for larger and larger canvases. It is as watchable today as it was 43 years ago and has lost nothing of its impact and style. If that is not the sign of a truly great piece of cinema I don't know what is. For a devotee of the Spaghetti Western genre, this is where it all begins.

Notes

1. Although referred to as "the man with no name," Eastwood's character is addressed as Joe in the movie.
2. This prologue is now available on the Special Edition released in 2005.

CHAPTER 3

For a Few Dollars More (1965)

(Constantin Film Produktion, Produzioni Europee Associati, Arturo González Producciones Cinematográficas; released in the United States by United Artists)
Original Title: *Per qualche dollaro in più*
Director: Sergio Leone
Story and Screenplay: Sergio Leone
Screenplay: Fulvio Morsella, Luciano Vincenzoni
Producers: Arturo González, Alberto Grimaldi
Music: Ennio Morricone
Cinematography: Massimo Dallamano
Editing: Eugenio Alabiso, Giorgio Serrallonga
Cast: Clint Eastwood (Manco), Lee Van Cleef (Col. Douglas Mortimer), Gian Maria Volonté (El Indio [The Indian]), Mario Brega (Nino, Member of Indio's Gang), Luigi Pistilli (Groggy, Member of Indio's Gang), Aldo Sambrell (Cuchillio), Klaus Kinski (Juan Wild, The Hunchback), Benito Stefanelli (Luke "Hughie"), Luis Rodríguez (Manuel, Member of Indio's Gang), Panos Papadopulos (Sancho Perez), Mara Krupp (Mary, Hotel Manager's Beautiful Wife), Roberto Camardiel (Tucumcari, Station Clerk), Joseph Egger (Old Prophet), Tomás Blanco (Tucumcari Sheriff), Lorenzo Robledo (Tomaso, Indio's Traitor), Sergio Mendizábal (Tucumcari Bank Manager), Dante Maggio (Carpenter in Cell with El Indio), Diana Rabito (Calloway's Beautiful Girl in Tub), Giovanni Tarallo (Santa Cruz Telegraphist), Mario Meniconi (Train Conductor), José Marco ("Baby" Red Cavanaugh), Antoñito Ruiz (Fernando), José Terrón (Guy Calloway), Román Ariznavarreta (Half-Shaved Bounty Hunter), Ricardo Palacios (Tucumcari Saloon Keeper), Carlo Simi (El Paso Bank Manager), Enrique Santiago (Miguel, Member of Indio's Gang), Guillermo Méndez (White Rocks Sheriff), Nazzareno Natale (Paco, Member of Indio's Gang), Werner Abrolat (Slim, Member of Indio's Gang), Frank Braña (Blackie, Member of Indio's Gang), José Canalejas (Chico, Member of Indio's Gang), Antonio Molino Rojo (Frisco, Member of Indio's Gang), Eduardo García

(Member of Indio's Gang), Rosemary Dexter (Mortimer's Sister), Peter Lee Lawrence (Mortimer's Brother-in-Law), Diana Faenza (Tomaso's Wife), Francesca Leone (Tomaso's Baby), Jesús Guzmán (Carpetbagger on Train), Kurt Zips (Hotel Manager), Maurizio Graf (The Balladeer [voice]), Sergio Leone (Whistling Bounty Hunter [voice]).

Voice Dubs: Dubbing actor (followed by screen actor in parentheses): Emilio Cigoli (Lee Van Cleef), Dhia Cristiani (Mara Krupp), Lauro Gazzolo (Joseph Egger), Nando Gazzolo (Gian Maria Volonté), Pino Locchi (Benito Stefanelli), Bruno Persa (Klaus Kinski), Enrico Maria Salerno (Clint Eastwood).

Budget: $750,000

Gross: $15,000,000 (USA)

Release Dates: Italy (December 18, 1965); USA (May 10, 1967)

Running Time: 132 minutes

Sound Mix: Mono (Western Electric Sound System)

Color: Technicolor

Aspect Ratio: 2.35: 1

Availability: DVD (Fox Searchlight); Blu-ray (Fox Searchlight)

The second in the Dollars trilogy, *For a Few Dollars More* is overall an even better film than its excellent predecessor. Usually overlooked due to being sandwiched between the milestone *A Fistful of Dollars* and the magnificent *The Good, the Bad, and the Ugly*, *For a Few Dollars More* benefits from a larger budget, a longer running time, more stylish direction, and better performances. It also more clearly presents Leone's contradictory vision as a filmmaker, wavering from traditional narrative, to wry satire, to dark fatalism.

Even before the credit sequence, Leone presents a lone rider in long shot, surrounded by negative space, looking tiny from the perspective of a sniper, who shoots him dead off his horse. That immediate, jarring moment is what leads into this film's credits. A title card flashes on the screen which states: "Where life had no value, death, sometimes, had its price. That is why the bounty killers appeared." This explains that the unknown tiny figure of a man who is killed in the long shot that opens the film is the likely victim of a bounty hunter. This sets the precedent for what follows.

We are first introduced to Colonel Mortimer (Lee Van Cleef) who forces a train to stop by pulling the emergency cord, gets off, and kills Guy Calloway (José Terrón) for a $1,000 bounty. Mortimer's character is immediately defined in this scene. His human prey escapes through a window, mounts his horse, and tries to flee. Mortimer goes outside, opens the pack on his own horse, and reveals several firearms. He grabs one, aims, and shoots the man's horse dead. Leone films this in a long shot from the shooter's perspective. When Calloway stands up and faces Mortimer, the director switches to close-ups. Calloway is shot but not killed. He gets up and begins shooting at Mortimer, but he is too far away

Poster for *For a Few Dollars More.*

for his pistol shots to be effective. He keeps moving closer as Mortimer patiently puts together a gun that has the necessary range and shoots Calloway dead. He then collects the bounty.

Mortimer then inquires about a criminal by the name of "Baby" Red Cavanaugh (José Marco), who has a $2,000 bounty. He is told where Cavanaugh is, but he is also told that another man inquired about him recently. The man's name is Manco[1] (Clint Eastwood).

Eastwood's character of Manco is not specifically the same character as Joe in *A Fistful of Dollars*. The previous film had been produced by Jolly Films; however, after a falling out with Sergio Leone, they were not involved in the sequel, and Alberto Grimaldi produced the film. Jolly Films sued, claiming rights to the character, but it was decided in court that the rudiments of the western gunfighter was part of the public domain and one could not copyright the manner of such a character. Thus, it cannot be legally considered that Manco is the same as Joe in *A Fistful of Dollars*.

Manco manages to catch up with Red Cavanaugh first, so we are allowed to witness his method after having been introduced to Mortimer's. Manco is more pragmatic. He interrupts Cavanaugh's card game and singlehandedly deals five cards for himself and Cavanaugh, who is more intrigued than angered. He draws three kings. Manco shows three aces.

> Cavanaugh: What are we playing for?
>
> Manco: Your life.

In filming this scene, Leone uses mostly close-ups, cutting from Manco's dealing hand, to his face, to Cavanaugh's bemused expression. Occasional, brief cuts to others involved in the game are used as dressing. We are reminded that Manco interrupted the game of several people, not just the one on whom he's fixated. Manco's very presence is imposing enough to keep all at bay while he patiently deals a game of stud between himself and the head of the table.

Cavanaugh prepares to draw, but he is thwarted by Manco who responds by wrestling the man down the stairs after blocking his attempts to strike. Manco chops Cavanaugh on each side of his neck. This martial arts–derived reaction is an interesting element to this character that had been absent in the previous film.

When Manco has beaten Cavanaugh and has him standing groggily against the bar, he is approached from behind by three of his bounty's men standing at the saloon doors. In the first action that completely parallels the actions of Joe in *A Fistful of Dollars*, Manco turns, fires three quick shots by hammering his pistol, and the men are quickly and efficiently killed. Rather than fall dead just outside the doors, the bodies of the three men propel backward several feet into the street; this is another example of the director's method of presenting the violent sequences in his films with something outside the expected and conventional, even so marginal as how peripheral characters die.

Mortimer is the next to be spotlighted. The real bounty for both men is the notorious El Indio (Gian Maria Volonté). Mortimer displays his own pragmatism by trying to get to El Indio by confronting one of his gang. His confrontation with the man they call Wild (also known as "the hunchback" and played

Eastwood in *For a Few Dollars More*.

by Klaus Kinski) is more confrontational and brutal than a mere interruption of a poker game. Mortimer stands close to Wild and strikes a match on his face to light a cigarette. An angry Wild blows out the match. Mortimer then takes Wild's cigarette and uses it to light his own. Wild goes for his gun more than once but is stopped by his men. He then walks away in a trembling rage, and a bartender warns Mortimer that Wild will not forget, and will seek revenge. Mortimer exhibits no concern. He has sent his message to El Indio.

Again it is the close-ups and quick edits that add more power to this scene. The languid expression on Mortimer and the shocked anger on Wild, his face twitching with rage, are clearly displayed as their faces fill the screen. Meanwhile, occasional cutaways to Manco standing at the saloon doors, witnessing the event, promises a confrontation between the two men.

One of the highlights in *For a Few Dollars More* is the inevitable confrontation between Manco and Colonel Mortimer, which happens fairly early in the movie. We have already been fully introduced to each man and their methods, and it gets to the point in the narrative where the only logical circumstance is for one to eliminate the other or for them to join forces. The latter seems unlikely, as both appear to be loners who would fiercely avoid collaboration with anyone.

Leone sets the confrontation between Manco and Mortimer outside the saloon on the street, with nobody watching, framing the situation as a classic western movie showdown. It begins as satire as each man scuffs the toe of the other's boot, first Manco scraping the heel of his on the toe of Mortimer's, then Mortimer responding in kind. It almost appears like the reciprocal comic battles

Lee Van Cleef.

of Laurel and Hardy. The men venture into the street. Manco shoots Mortimer's hat off his head. When Mortimer goes to pick it up, Manco shoots it farther down the street. This happens several times, with Mortimer's anger building not unlike Wild's in the previous scene. Leone shoots much of this from Manco's perspective, sometimes from just behind Manco so both figures are visible within the frame, Mortimer well into the background. Occasional medium shots give us a look at Mortimer's building anger. In response, Mortimer shoots Manco's hat off of his head, it flies into the air, and Mortimer continues to shoot at it, keeping it propelled toward the sky. Each man succeeds in impressing the other, and they decide to defy their own loner instincts and team up.

The dynamic the script calls for is between an older gunfighter and a younger one. Leone wanted to cast Henry Fonda (who was several years Eastwood's senior) in the role, but even with the larger budget, he could not meet Fonda's price. Lee Van Cleef plays the role well (referring to himself as approaching fifty), but in real life the actor was only forty and a mere five years older than Eastwood. Still, the acting of each makes this dynamic work effectively.

Van Cleef had not made a film in three years and had been concentrating on TV work when he was hired to play Mortimer in *For a Few Dollars More*. Having been in films since appearing in the classic *High Noon* (1952), Van Cleef had worked with directors like Fred Zinnemann and John Ford, usually playing bit roles, and expected his part in this movie would only take a few days. Upon arriving on the set, Van Cleef was shocked—and pleasantly surprised—when he discovered he would have a co-starring role. Van Cleef knew Eastwood, having appeared with him on a *Rawhide* episode, and despite his being pleased with such a large, important role, he still expressed misgivings about the production. Van Cleef had small roles in films with top-flight directors and recognized a shoddy production situation. Eastwood reassured him and told him to arrange for a screening of *A Fistful of Dollars*. Van Cleef did, understood what the filmmakers were doing, and brought to this movie a standout performance. Steely eyed, mostly expressionless, sucking on a curved pipe, Mortimer is cool and collected but not above reacting with aggressive, brutal force. His manner hints of a painful backstory. The dynamic between Mortimer and Manco is immediately intriguing. They are both vigilantes for money, both going after the same man, and are both cold and cynical.

It is decided that Manco would infiltrate El Indio's gang in an effort to get closer. He helps one of his men escape prison, is admitted to the gang, and joins them when they carry off a safe that is said to contain "almost a million dollars." When they arrive in the border town of Agua Caliente, Mortimer is there waiting, indicating that he can open the safe. Wild, however, recognizes him from the encounter in the bar and challenges him. Wild is easily killed, impressing El Indio, who is further pleased when Mortimer is able to open the safe without the use of explosives. The plan is for El Indio to keep the money over a month, and distribute it evenly after the excitement of the robbery has dissipated. Manco and Mortimer later attempt to steal the money but are caught by El Indio's men, beaten, and tied up. The men are quietly set free by Nino (Mario Brega), upon El Indio's orders. El Indio tells his men the prisoners have escaped and sends his gang in pursuit. His intention is for his men to kill Manco and Mortimer, after which El Indio plans to kill his gang and keep all of the money for himself and Nino. However, one of the gang, Groggy (Luigi Pistilli), figures out the plan, kills Nino, and plans to kill El Indio. Discovering that Mortimer and Manco have already stolen the money from where it had been hidden, he is convinced by El Indio to join forces with him, kill the two men, and split the money. Meanwhile, Manco and Mortimer are confronted by El Indio's gang who are killed off one by one in the same easy, efficient manner as had been displayed throughout the film.

This leads to the final confrontation where Leone once again frames the action in the same manner as a classic western but puts his own cinematic spin on the proceedings. A running gag in the story is that whenever El Indio kills someone, he takes out a pocket watch that plays a tune, and when the music ends, the victim is killed. The watch has a picture of a woman in it, but her identity is never revealed. Mortimer shoots Groggy but has his gun shot out of his hand by El Indio. El Indio takes out the pocket watch. As the music plays, Manco appears with an identical watch, playing the same music. A shot of Mortimer reaching in his pocket tells us that Manco had taken the watch from him. Manco has El Indio covered with a rifle and gives his gunbelt to Mortimer, evening the odds. Manco then sits on the sidelines patiently, allowing the confrontation between Mortimer and El Indio to take place. The music from the watch concludes, Mortimer draws first, and El Indio is killed. Mortimer then reveals to Manco that the woman in the watch is his sister, whom El Indio had murdered. Having gotten his revenge, he allows Manco to keep the reward money. Manco puts the bodies in the wagon and begins adding up the reward money for each, when the wounded Groggy approaches from behind. Manco turns and kills him, adding him to the wagon.

> Mortimer (having heard the gunshot): Trouble, boy?
>
> Manco: I was having trouble with my adding, but it's all right now.

Leone again visits classic western motifs by showing Mortimer riding off into the sunset, his figure in the distance, surrounded by the same negative space as the hapless victim that introduced the movie. Manco rides off in a wagon, prepared to collect his bounty. Leone never reveals what is done with the stolen bank money.

Edward Gallafent stated in *Clint Eastwood: Filmmaker and Star*:

> Whereas in the central act of *A Fistful of Dollars* a memory of the
> past is behind an act of rescue, the comparable impulse in this film,
> a redemption in the present, again relating to a past moment where
> nobody was around to help a woman, is now a response to an atroc-
> ity that can be revenge but not redeemed in the present. There is no
> woman in this film through whom the past can be given symbolic
> reembodiment and release. It is also significant that the relationship
> to the past and the woman in it is given here not to the figure played
> by Eastwood, but to another kind of American.

Much of *For a Few Dollars More* was filmed in Almeria, Spain, its location
effectively designed by Carlo Simi. Leone used the expanse of the set effectively
with long shots evening out his penchant for many close-ups. The same location
would be used again for the next film, *The Good, the Bad, and the Ugly*. Still
standing at the time of this writing, it has become a popular tourist attraction.

Ennio Morricone's music is once again utilized for maximum effect, and
Leone also investigates more possibilities with sound in this movie. During the
confrontation between Manco and Mortimer, the shooting of the hats is not
only punctuated by the sound of the gunshots, but of a whistling that accompanies that hat's movement. Perhaps the most effective use of sound is El Indio's
pocket watch tune, which is made even more eerie when its conclusion results
in murder, including the murder of a young woman and her baby in another
brutal defiance of Hollywood convention. Morricone's score, and Leone's use
of sound, seem even more intrinsic to the action than it had been in *A Fistful
of Dollars*.

This defiance of convention had some critics confused. Roger Ebert wrote
in the *Chicago Sun Times*:

> Here is a gloriously greasy, sweaty, hairy, bloody and violent West-
> ern. It is delicious. *For a Few Dollars More*, like all of the grand and
> corny Westerns Hollywood used to make, is composed of situations
> and not plots. Plots were dangerous because if a kid went out to get
> some popcorn he might miss something. So Westerns had situations,
> instantly recognizable. The man in the black hat strikes a match on
> the suspenders of a tough guy at the bar. Two gunmen face each
> other at each end of a long alley. *For a Few Dollars More* has lots of
> stuff like that, but it's on a larger, more melodramatic scale, if that's
> possible. Shoot-outs aren't over in a few minutes like they were in
> *High Noon*. They last forever. This is a sequel to *A Fistful of Dollars*,
> which I didn't see but wish I had. Both films were shot in Italy, with
> English-speaking actors in the leads and Italians in the bit parts with
> dubbed dialog.

Ebert, then a young critic in his first year reviewing movies, appears impressed by the style and presentation but does not seem to completely grasp the satire or the purposeful defiance of convention. In hindsight, we can see how *For a Few Dollars More* continued from the previous movie to redefine the western genre, and how Eastwood's screen persona was established (and in contrast to the TV character by which he'd become famous).[2]

Bosley Crowther of the *New York Times* seemed to understand the intentions somewhat better, having seen—and reviewed—*A Fistful of Dollars*:

> The cool-cat image of a Western gun-slinger that was studiously fabricated by Clint Eastwood in *A Fistful of Dollars*, under the direction of Sergio Leone, is repeated by Mr. Eastwood in the aptly titled *For a Few Dollars More*, which broke loose with some Fourth of July fireworks at the Trans-Lux West and other theaters yesterday. Everyone susceptible to the illusion that shooting and killing with fancy flourishes are fun can indulge his bloodlust to the fullest at this synthetic Italian-Spanish-made Western film. Once again Mr. Leone has filled his plushly colored screen and his deliberately calculated sound-track with conglomerate stimuli that agitate moods of dread and danger, of morbid menace and suspense, and then erupt in cascades of vivid violence, fistfights, shootings and death . . . the dynamics of it are in the freedom and ferocity with which Mr. Leone piles violence upon violence and charges the screen with the hideous fantasies of sudden death. In the close-up faces of his ugly ruffians, highlighted and shadowed in burnished hues, and in the ominous thump of drums and wail of trumpets that preface his menace scenes, he prepares us for the violent explosions that mark the deadly circuit of pursuit. In the bark of guns, the whine of bullets and the spinning bodies of men mortally hit, he provides the aural and visual stimulation for an excitement of morbid lust.

Lee Van Cleef's character is every bit as charismatic as Eastwood's and does just as much to advance the narrative. He is never subordinate, and he is allowed many scenes in which Eastwood does not appear at all. Van Cleef, who would return in *The Good, the Bad, and the Ugly*, would forever be grateful for the push his career got from these opportunities. Mortimer is given much more depth with his backstory, while Manco is only in it for the money once again, and in the end, it is Mortimer who shoots the bad guy as Manco looks on. But it is Eastwood's screen persona that was becoming established for subsequent starring films—and iconic performances. Richard Schickel stated in his biography of Eastwood:

> The first film sketched, in bold strokes, a screen character—basically a self-contained ironist, worldly-wise but not world-weary, determined

to pursue his destiny and equally determined not to define it, or himself verbally—that was also capable of enrichment. There is something of his Leone character in everything he's done since. The "dyin' ain't much of a livin'" Clint, the "Make my day" Clint, have their beginnings in the brutally frank figure who comically tallies his profits at the end of *For a Few Dollars More*.

Rawhide was coming to a conclusion on television when *For a Few Dollars More* was released in Italy to the same positive reaction that *A Fistful of Dollars* had enjoyed. Eastwood was happy to leave the stressful grind of a weekly TV series and a character he no longer enjoyed playing. Furthermore, the success of his second Leone western proved that his first success was no fluke. The second film, with its larger budget and more expansive production, grossed somewhat more than its predecessor and proved that Clint Eastwood was an actor who could carry a film. As a result, when Leone prepared a third western, initially titled *The Magnificent Rogues*, he received further backing by the American studio United Artists, who recognized that Eastwood, and Leone, had proven themselves to be a bankable investment.

Eastwood's shrewdness might not have been as commonly known at this time, but in retrospect we can appreciate the fact that the actor's insight was already brimming with ideas for his future, both immediate and long term. He realized that the Leone westerns were a stepping-stone to even greater success in his own country; he also understood that just being an actor was limiting his scope from both a creative and financial perspective.

While contemplating future possibilities and preparing to work in another Leone film, Clint Eastwood was contacted by producer Dino DeLaurentiis, who was putting together a collection of short films within the context of a feature—titled *The Witches*—to star his wife, Silvana Mangano, in an attempt to revive the actress's career. Each vignette would have its own director, cast, and story. Due to his popularity with Italian audiences, Eastwood agreed to appear in the film. His pay was $20,000 and his own Ferrari. Eastwood enjoyed the experience, especially being directed by Vittorio De Sica, whose films *The Bicycle Thief* (1948) and *Shoeshine* (1946) are among the quintessential examples of Italian neorealism in cinema. He got along well with Mangano (who spoke fluent English), and with De Sica, who praised Eastwood in the press as a "fine, sensitive actor." The film achieved little success, but Eastwood felt he benefited from the experience. He had the Ferrari shipped to New York during production and, upon his return, drove it home to California with his wife, the sports car filled with their luggage. According to Richard Schickel's biography, Eastwood stated, "[W]ith all that luggage we looked like *The Grapes of Wrath*. Of course the vehicle was different."

Eastwood then prepared to return to Italy yet again to start his third and final film with Sergio Leone. *The Magnificent Rogues* was, of course, to later be known as *The Good, the Bad, and the Ugly*. And while *A Fistful of Dollars* and *For a Few Dollars More* were progressively brilliant, *The Good, the Bad, and the Ugly* was a superior culmination that not only effectively concluded the trilogy, but continues in the twenty-first century to be one of the most noted European films and most beloved and respected westerns in all of cinema.

Notes

1. *Manco* is Spanish for "single-armed," and throughout the film, Eastwood performs nearly all actions with one hand and keeping his right tucked under his poncho, resting on his gun.

2. In fairness, Ebert later changed his opinion on this movie.

CHAPTER 4

The Good, the Bad, and the Ugly (1966)

(Produzioni Europee Associati, Arturo González Producciones Cinematográficas, Constantin Film Produktion; released in the United States by United Artists)

Original Italian Title: *Il buono, il brutto, il cattivo*

Director: Sergio Leone

Story and Screenplay: Sergio Leone and Luciano Vincenzoni; English version by Mickey Knox

Producer: Alberto Grimaldi

Music: Ennio Morricone

Cinematography: Tonino Delli Colli

Film Editing: Eugenio Alabiso, Nino Baragli

Cast: Eli Wallach (Tuco); Clint Eastwood (Blondie); Lee Van Cleef (Sentenza / Angel Eyes); Aldo Giuffrè (Alcoholic Union Captain); Luigi Pistilli (Father Pablo Ramirez); Rada Rassimov (Maria); Enzo Petito (Storekeeper); Claudio Scarchilli (Mexican Peon); John Bartha (Sheriff); Livio Lorenzon (Baker); Antonio Casale (Jackson); Angelo Novi (Monk); Antonio Casas (Stevens); Chelo Alonso (Stevens' Wife); Antoñito Ruiz (Stevens' Youngest Son); Al Mulock (One-Armed Bounty Hunter); Sergio Mendizábal (Blonde Bounty Hunter); Anotonio Molino Rojo (Capt. Harper); Mario Brega (Cpl. Wallace); José Terrón (Shorty); William Conroy (Confederate Soldier); Tony Di Mitiri (Deputy); Jesús Guzmán (Hotel Owner); Víctor Israel (Sergeant at Confederate Fort); Ricardo Palacios (Bartender in Socorro); Benito Stefanelli, Aldo Sambrell, Romano Puppo, Luigi Ciavarro (Members of Angel Eyes's gang); Aysanoa Runachagua (Pistolero Recruited by Tuco in the Cave); Fortunato Arena (1st Sombrero Onlooker at Tucho's 1st Hanging); Amerigo Castrighella (2nd Sombrero Onlooker at Tucho's 1st Hanging); Attilio Dottesio (3rd Sombrero Onlooker at Tucho's 1st Hanging); Veriano Ginesi (Bald Onlooker at Tucho's 1st Hanging); Saturno Cerra, Román Ariznavarreta, Frank Braña, Nazzareno Natale, Enrique Santiago (Bounty Hunters).

Voice Dubs: Carlo Romano (Eli Wallach), Enrico Maria Salerno (Clint East-
   wood), Emilio Cigoli (Lee Van Cleef), Nando Gazzolo (Luigi Pistilli), Pino
   Locchi (Aldo Giuffrè), Glauco Onorato (Al Mulock), Luigi Pavese (An-
   tonio Casas), Nino Pavese (John Bartha), Bruno Persa (Víctor Israel),
   Mario Pisu (Livio Lorenzon), Rita Savagnone (Rada Rassimov), Renato
   Turi (Mario Brega).
Budget: $1,200,000 (estimated)
Gross: $6,100,000 (USA)
Release Dates: Italy (December 23, 1966); USA (December 29, 1967)
Running Time: 161 minutes[1]
Sound Mix: Mono
Color: Technicolor
Aspect Ratio: 2.35: 1
Availability: DVD (MGM); Blu-ray (MGM)

The Good, the Bad, and the Ugly is the perfect culmination of the Dollars trilogy, remaining one of the most brilliantly filmed, scored, and acted films in the western genre. As the other two films, this one revisits conventions as well as defies them, uses close-ups and expansive long shots intermittently and effectively, and offers a level of violence that was shocking in its brutality, but, in hindsight, is a progressive depiction that inspired subsequent films, including those Eastwood later directed.

As the film was being planned, a deal was struck with the American company United Artists who had seen how lucrative Eastwood's previous two movies had been. The agreement with United Artists was for a million-dollar budget with the studio advancing $500,000 up front in return for 50 percent of the box office outside of Italy. The total budget would eventually extend to the neighborhood of $1.3 million. Leone and Vincenzoni collaborated on the story and screenplay from an idea Vincenzoni had. His co-writer also recommended writers Agenore Incrocci and Furio Scarpelli, whose work mostly specialized in comedy, believing they could add to the wry sense of humor of the other films. Leone was displeased with their ideas, later claiming he might have used one line of theirs. According to Christopher Frayling's book *Sergio Leone: Something to Do with Death*, Leone stated, "I couldn't use a single thing they'd written. It was the grossest deception of my life."

The setting is the Civil War, making it a prequel to the two previous films in the Dollars trilogy. The opening scene presents three bounty hunters in close-up approaching a building in a desolate western setting. Leone concentrates on the facial features of each man, editing in close-up between them. The men enter a building, gunshots are heard, and a fourth man bursts through a window and escapes on horseback. The camera pans back to show two of the bounty hunters

Poster for *The Good, the Bad, and the Ugly.*

dead, and a third one alive but missing an arm. A title on the screen identifies the escaped man as "The Ugly." We soon learn he is Tuco (Eli Wallach).

The next scene shows us "The Bad," known as Angel Eyes (Lee Van Cleef) interrogating a former Confederate soldier, Stevens (Antonio Casas), about a man named Bill Carson, who knows the whereabouts of hidden Confederate gold. Angel Eyes kills Stevens, collects the bounty, and kills his employer.

As with *For a Few Dollars More*, Eastwood is not in these opening scenes. Van Cleef gets another co-starring role, and Eli Wallach is added with top billing and more footage than either of the other actors. Van Cleef told Patrick McGilligan for the book *Clint: The Life and Legend*, "the only way I got a role in this movie was because they forgot to kill me off in the last one." Eastwood showed some concern of being upstaged, pointing out to the director that he was a loner in the first, a duo in the second, and now a trio. It was nothing personal against the actors. He continued to get along well with Van Cleef and traveled to the Madrid location with Wallach.

Eastwood plays Blondie, "The Good," and his first appearance is to rescue Tuco from yet another group of bounty hunters who ambush him. Blondie appears, challenges the group, outdraws them, and kills them all. Tuco's elation soon turns to rage when he discovers Blondie did that simply to collect the $2,000 bounty on Tuco himself. Just as Tuco is about to be hanged, Blondie helps him escape, the two split the reward money, and they team up with ideas for more money-making schemes. However, Tuco's personality becomes an annoyance, so Blondie leaves him alone and penniless in the desert.

There is an interesting comparison-contrast to the Blondie and Tuco characters. While Manco and Mortimer in *For a Few Dollars More* had some vague differences but even more similarities, Blondie and Tuco are markedly different. Blondie, as with Eastwood's other characters, is a tall, looming presence whose charisma bleeds through a strict economy of movements and expressions. Tuco is small, feisty, and manic. His character sputters and splatters through his scenes with jittery movements and a snarling vocal delivery. Wallach, a veteran of the Actors' Studio, was already a respected character actor, having appeared in such top films as Elia Kazan's *Baby Doll* (1956); John Huston's *The Misfits* (1961), penned by Arthur Miller and noted as the final film of both Clark Gable and Marilyn Monroe; and Sam Peckinpah's *The Magnificent Seven* (1960), from which he seems to derive his character for this film. Eastwood's concern about being upstaged was fully warranted, but he holds his own against Wallach's more blatant histrionics. The character of Blondie is, like the characters in the previous films, a cynic with no real allegiance to anyone. He is more interested in the payoff than the person. His presence is imposing. Eastwood anchors the scenes in which he appears opposite Wallach.

Eastwood in *The Good, the Bad, and the Ugly*.

Tuco survives his desert ordeal and relentlessly searches for Blondie. Once Blondie is found, Tuco forces him to march across a blistering desert, causing him to collapse from the heat. Tuco is ready to shoot the dehydrated Blondie when he is distracted by a runaway carriage. He manages to stop the carriage and finds a dying man inside. The man is Bill Carson (Antonio Casale) who promises to reveal the whereabouts of the $200,000 of Confederate gold, which he says is buried in a cemetery. The cemetery is revealed but not the name on the grave. Tuco runs to get water, but when he returns, Carson is dead and Blondie is lying next to him. Blondie reveals that Carson told him the name on the grave. Tuco needs that information, so he gives Blondie the water, and the unlikely partnership is formed in order to find the money.

It is interesting that the only allegiance Eastwood's character is allowed in these films is one of necessity for monetary gain. It is evident that the Blondie and Tuco partnership consists of two men who hate each other, who are unconcerned with killing one another, but each of whom needs information from the other. The trajectory of Eastwood's subsequent career would feature a series of roles in which his character would balk at having to partner up with anyone.

Blondie and Tuco go to a mission on the frontier, where Tuco's brother is the priest. They don Confederate uniforms and leave, but they are captured by

Eastwood and Eli Wallach.

Union soldiers and taken to a prison camp. At the roll call, when the name Bill Carson is called, Tuco is talked into answering to it by Blondie. Angel Eyes, now a sergeant in the Union army, hears the name, realizing Carson is the one who knows the whereabouts of the Confederate gold. He has Tuco tortured for the information, and Tuco eventually gives up what he knows. Blondie knows the rest, and Angel Eyes realizes attempts to retrieve it the same way will not likely net positive results. Blondie is tougher, more stoic, and a more wily adversary who could easily turn the tables on whatever methods Angel Eyes might attempt in order to extract any information. He instead offers him half of the loot in exchange for what he knows. As a result, another allegiance is formed out of necessity.

The brutality of Tuco's torture scene was especially jarring when the film was first released and remains among the most violent scenes in any of Leone's films. The brutality is essentially just a beating, but it is augmented with other methods of hands-on cruelty, such as when Leone offers a close-up of the torturer's thumbs pressing deeply into Tuco's eyes. Leone's penchant for close-ups enhances the violence of a scene such as this. Tuco's gurgling cries of pain, his defiance turning to fear, the torturer's lack of emotion, and Angel Eyes's relaxed manner combine to make this scene resonate with the viewer.

Once Blondie and Angel Eyes form their partnership, Tuco remains a Union prisoner and is put on a train and chained to a guard (Mario Brega). In another of the most impressive scenes in the movie, Tuco grabs the guard, jumps from the train, and lands hard on the desert ground, smashing the guard's head with a rock. Finding no key to unlock the chains, Tuco tries to smash them with rocks but to no avail. He then drags the guard over the tracks with the chain along the rail. A train eventually comes by and breaks the chain, freeing him.

In another brilliantly presented scene, Leone uses a wide shot to display the jump from the train. The noise and spectacle of the train go by in the background, while in the foreground Tuco kills the guard. We do not see him drag the larger man to the tracks. The scene cuts to his already being there, a sleeping Tuco waiting, presumably for some time, in the hot sun until another train comes by. Once Tuco is freed, Leone offers us a shot beneath the moving train, the dead guard's body being dragged along the tracks. Tuco races to the back of the train and jumps aboard.

This was a particularly dangerous sequence, almost costing Eli Wallach his life. Neither the actor, the director, nor any of the crew was aware of the heavy iron steps that extended from each of the trains' boxcars. If Wallach had stood up at the wrong time as the train passed, the steps could have decapitated him.

Another highlight featuring Wallach soon follows. Tuco makes his way to an evacuated town where Blondie and Angel Eyes have also fled. Unbeknownst to Tuco, the bounty hunter from the beginning of the film, who survived with a severed arm, has been trailing him. He corners Tuco, who is taking a bath. He makes a speech about how he's had to live without one of his arms, and now he is getting his revenge. Tuco shoots a hidden rifle and kills the man, stating, "If you're going to shoot, then shoot! Don't talk!"

Blondie, alerted by the gunshot, walks in and finds Tuco. Making a strategic move, Blondie asks Tuco to partner up with him, kill Angel Eyes and his men, and get the Confederate gold. They manage to kill off all of the men, but Angel Eyes escapes. Tuco and Blondie head toward the cemetery but are captured en route by Union soldiers. Agreeing to join the Union army, Tuco and Blondie dynamite[2] a bridge separating the Union and Confederate soldiers, which causes them to disperse. Tuco reveals the name of the cemetery, Sad Hill, and Blondie indicates that the grave where the gold is buried belongs to Arch Stanton. The next morning, Tuco steals a horse and heads to the cemetery alone. In one of the most beautiful long shots in the movie, Leone shows Wallach running through the cemetery, graves occupying most of the negative space, the music swelling up to indicate Tuco's excitement. When he arrives at the grave marked Arch Stanton, he giggles with excitement, a close-up showing a manic look of euphoria in his eyes. As he begins digging with a piece of wood, a shovel is tossed down. He looks up and finds Blondie, who tells him, at gunpoint, to continue digging.

Angel Eyes suddenly appears, with a gun on both men. When the grave is dug up, there is no money in the wooden box, just a decaying skeleton.[3] Blondie has not revealed the true whereabouts of the gold. A three-way duel is agreed upon.

The narrative shows Leone exploring some of the traditional elements of the more conventional western movie with a classic showdown situation to resolve the narrative conflict. He uses it to present more of Blondie's strategic thinking. Blondie quickly outdraws and fires on Angel Eyes, but when Tuco fires, he finds his gun is empty. Blondie, who has killed Angel Eyes, reveals he had emptied it during the night, foreseeing that Tuco may very well set out on his own for the gold. Leone shoots the duel by editing among close-ups of each man's eyes, revealing their character and their feelings before the first shot is fired.

Blondie indicates that the unmarked grave next to Arch Stanton holds the Confederate gold. Tuco digs it up and giggles maniacally as he pulls out several bags heavy with gold. He looks up and, in a brilliantly framed shot, sees a hangman's noose that Blondie has prepared for him. Leone shoots this with the rope hanging in the foreground, the noose opening perfectly framing Eli Wallach in the background.

Tuco is forced to stand unsteadily on the grave marker and tighten the noose around his neck. Blondie takes his half of the money, leaves the rest for Tuco, and rides off. Tuco is helpless, unable to move without hanging himself. He screams for Blondie repeatedly but to no immediate avail. Suddenly, Blondie shoots the rope, and Tuco falls. Blondie rides off as Tuco hollers behind him, "You know what you are? Just a dirty son of a bitch!"

The Good, the Bad, and the Ugly is a masterpiece of filmmaking, with Sergio Leone's direction at its most visually creative, from the close-ups of the bounty hunters that open the film, to the beautiful long shot of Blondie riding off alone. In many scenes, especially those taking place with the Union army, there is a great deal of movement in the negative space, filling the background, while we concentrate on the main characters in the foreground. A dinner table sequence between Tuco and Angel Eyes, before the brutal torture sequence, is a nicely composed shot of Van Cleef in the foreground on the side, and Tuco in the background facing front. Leone was said to have a real deep interest in art, which might have somewhat informed his choices regarding shot composition and how to frame the action most effectively. Other studies have pointed out Leone's interest in opera, his cutting between close-ups and long shots showing terror, violence, and scenes with an elegiac grace. As cinema's core is a series of images, Leone's bleak, wide canvas, with rugged, inappropriate elements, are examples of surrealistic beauty. Clint Eastwood's later work will exhibit how much he had learned about spectacle from Leone.

Along with being a masterfully shot and edited film, there are ideas that have been inspired by the previous efforts. The shooting of hats in *For a Few*

Dollars More is revisited in a scene where Blondie fans the hammer of his weapon and rapidly shoots the hats off several men, each shown in close-up having his hat shot off in a series of quick rhythmic edits.

Filming went from May to July 1966. Eastwood's salary grew larger. For this film, he received $250,000, another Ferrari, and 10 percent of the film's U.S. box office. Leone once again shot the film without sound, adding voices, music, and sound effects later. There were scenes excised from the American release that did appear in the Italian version. When these scenes were included for an American DVD in the 2000s, Eastwood and Wallach were hired to dub them in English nearly forty years after having made the movie. Lee Van Cleef died in 1989, so his part had to be voiced by Simon Prescott.

When *The Good, the Bad, and the Ugly* was released in December 1967, it enjoyed success at the box office, but criticism was mixed at best. Renata Adler of the *New York Times* called the film "the most expensive, pious and repellent movie in the history of its peculiar genre." Charles Champlin of the *Los Angeles Times* called it "The Bad, the Dull, and the Interminable." *Variety* said it was "dramatically feeble and offensively sadistic."

Times have changed and so has critical response to the movie. Richard Corliss and Richard Schickel in *Time* magazine considered it among the 100 greatest movies of the last century. Filmmaker Quentin Tarantino told Rob Turner of *Entertainment Weekly* that *The Good, the Bad, and the Ugly* was "the best-directed film of all time" and "the greatest achievement in the history of cinema." In *Empire* magazine's "The 500 Greatest Movies," *The Good, the Bad, and the Ugly* made number 25. In 2003, Roger Ebert revisited the film on his website, offering this review:

> When the movie opened in America in late 1967, not long after its predecessors, *A Fistful of Dollars* (1964) and *For a Few Dollars More* (1965), audiences knew they liked it, but did they know why? I saw it sitting in the front row of the balcony of the Oriental Theatre, whose vast wide screen was ideal for Leone's operatic compositions. Looking up my old review, I see I described a four-star movie but only gave it three stars, perhaps because it was a "spaghetti Western" and so could not be art.
>
> But art it is, summoned out of the imagination of Leone and painted on the wide screen so vividly that we forget what marginal productions these films were—that Clint Eastwood was a Hollywood reject, that budgetary restraints caused gaping continuity errors, that there wasn't a lot of dialogue because it was easier to shoot silent and fill the soundtrack with music and effects. There was even a pathetic attempt to make the films seem more American.
>
> Perhaps it is the subtly foreign flavor of the spaghetti trilogy, and especially the masterpiece *The Good, the Bad and the Ugly*, that suggests

the films come from a different universe than traditional Westerns. Instead of tame Hollywood extras from central casting, we get locals who must have been hired near the Spanish locations—men who look long-weathered by work and the sun. Yes, but Eastwood himself was to become an important director, and even then he must have sensed in Leone not just another purveyor of the Italian sword-and-sandal epics, but a man with passion.

Nineteen minutes were cut from the first release of *The Good, the Bad, and the Ugly*. But uncut versions of all of Leone's films are available on DVD, and gradually it becomes clear how good he really was.

Unfortunately, Clint Eastwood's and Sergio Leone's relationship barely made it through this film. Eastwood became tired of Leone's demanding methods; his penchant for many takes from several different angles would exhaust the actors working in the hot sun. Even during the dubbing session, Eastwood balked at being given a script to read from that was different than the shooting script. He demanded, and received, a shooting script to work from.

Sergio Leone wanted Eastwood to play the harmonica kid in *Once upon a Time in the West* (1968) and even flew to California to personally deliver the script to the actor. When Leone presented the story in person, the meeting went poorly. Eastwood's impatience with Leone's careful explanation of the slow-moving opening sequence put him off right away. Whenever he'd try to hurry Leone along, the director maintained his pace. Eastwood turned the role down, and Charles Bronson was eventually cast.

The opening scene of *Once upon a Time in the West* is one of the finest openings of any film, western or otherwise, European or American, and much of its impact is due to how slowly it is paced and how effectively Leone uses sound and almost no movement other than the camera's focus on the character. Eastwood may or may not have understood its brilliance when simply having it explained, but it appears that he simply wasn't interested in doing a fourth movie with the director and had his sights on other opportunities. Leone was unhappy, and when he made *Once upon a Time in America* (1984), he compared that film's star, Robert De Niro, favorably with Eastwood in interviews. Eastwood and Leone would make amends shortly before the director's death in 1989.

Discussing *The Good, the Bad, and the Ugly* with Gregory J. M. Castos for *Filmfax* magazine, Eli Wallach stated:

> Leone was very particular about how to make this film. He wanted it to have strong visual moments, and it did, like me about to be hanged, or the close-ups on the eyes. He used a lot of close-ups instead of dialogue. . . . When I met Leone, he was wearing a belt and suspenders. I thought, "How unusual that is!" So I told him I wanted

my character "Tuco" to dress that way. Leone's answer was that he wanted me to play this scummy outlaw with "no holster for his gun!" I asked, "Where do I carry the gun, then?" He explained, "You'll have a concealed gun tied to a rope; a lanyard, around your neck." "So," I asked, "the gun dangles between my legs, right?" He said, "Yes. When you want the gun you twist your shoulders and then the gun will be in your hands." I asked him to show me how I could shoot a gun this way. He said, "Like this!" He put the lanyard on, twisted his shoulder, and the gun hit him right in the groin! Undaunted, he said, "On second thought, just put the gun in your pocket."

Clint Eastwood had enjoyed success overseas, but in his own country his latest work was *Rawhide*. Being successful in a foreign market meant little to American film producers. Movie executives also were dismissive toward those they believed to be primarily TV actors, and thus few crossed over. Eastwood responded by forming his own company, and he made a deal with United Artists to co-produce the American-made western *Hang 'Em High*.

Notes

1. The 2003 DVD and Blu-ray of this film ran 179 minutes, with scenes from the Italian version that had not previously been included. It is this version that was screened for the chapter.

2. This film is set during the Civil War, and dynamite was not invented until 1867. The bridge was blown up prematurely in an erroneous call by a cameraman and had to be rebuilt and blown up again for the film.

3. The skeleton is real. In her will, a Spanish actress stipulated that she continue to appear in films, even after her death. The skeleton is her remains.

CHAPTER 5

Hang 'Em High (1968)

(A Leonard Freeman co-production with the Malpaso Company; released by United Artists)

Director: Ted Post
Screenplay: Mel Goldberg, Leonard Freeman
Producer: Leonard Freeman
Associate Producer: Irving L. Leonard
Supervising Producer: Robert Stambler
Music: Dominic Frontiere
Cinematography: Richard H. Kline, Leonard J. South
Editing: Gene Fowler Jr.
Cast: Clint Eastwood (Marshal Jed Cooper); Inger Stevens (Rachel Warren); Ed Begley (Captain Wilson); Pat Hingle (Judge Fenton); Ben Johnson (Marshal Dave Bliss); Charles McGraw (Sheriff Ray Calhoun); Ruth White (Madame "Peaches" Sophie); Bruce Dern (Miller); Alan Hale Jr. (Matt Stone); Arlene Golonka (Jennifer); L. Q. Jones (Loomis); Michael O'Sullivan (Francis Elroy Duffy); Joseph Sirola (Reno); Bob Steele (Jenkins); Bert Freed (Schmidt); Russell Thorson (Maddow); Ned Romero (Charlie Blackfoot); Jonathan Lippe (Tommy); Rick Gates (Ben); Bruce Scott (Billy Joe); Herbert Ellis (Swede); Joel Fluellen (Williams); Jack Ging (Marshal Ace Hayes); Robert B. Williams (Elwood); Tod Andrews (Defense Attorney); Mark Lenard (Prosecutor); Dennis Hopper (The Prophet); James MacArthur (The Preacher); Bill Zuckert (Sheriff); Hank Robinson (Deputy); Jimmie Booth (Stage Driver); Hal England (Brother); Tammy Locke (Little Girl); Paul Sorenson, James Westerfield, Harve Parry, Larry Blake (Prisoners); Roy Glenn, John Welsey (Guards); John Cochran (Jailer); Jack Gordon, Michael Jeffers, Jack Tornek (Hanging Spectators); Jeffrey Sayre, Richard Angarola, Ted Thorpe, Robert Jones, Barry Cahill, Dennis Dengate, Tony Di Milo, Richard Guizon (Townspeople).
Estimated Budget: $1,800,000
Estimated Gross: $6,800,000
Release Date: August 3, 1968

Running Time: 114 minutes
Sound Mix: Mono
Color: Deluxe
Aspect Ratio: 1.85: 1
Availability: DVD and Blu-ray (MGM)

Clint Eastwood had turned down a role in Sergio Leone's *Once upon a Time in the West*, partly due to wanting to explore other ideas, but also because the meeting between himself and Leone about that film's script went poorly. *Once upon a Time in the West* remains one of the finest progressive westerns of Leone's career. Some believe it to be his masterpiece.

Eastwood also turned down big studio productions where he'd be merely an actor for hire. He had just appeared opposite Richard Burton in the air force opus *Where Eagles Dare* (1968) and was therefore not interested when offered a role in *MacKenna's Gold*, which was to star Gregory Peck. His decision was sound, as *MacKenna's Gold* was a box office failure. Now with his own production company, Malpaso,[1] and a bit of box office clout, Eastwood's sights were on independent production. He looked over a few scripts and finally settled on a western co-written by producer Leonard Freeman, who had helped Eastwood set up Malpaso. Eastwood took what he learned from the western movies and TV shows in which he'd appeared, including *Rawhide* and the Leone westerns, and combined his frame of reference to inform what was to become *Hang 'Em High*.

Several different directors were considered, but Eastwood insisted on Ted Post, whose career was most extensively in television, including nearly thirty episodes of *Rawhide*. In an interview with the author, Post recalled:

> I had directed two feature pictures by then, but I did hundreds of TV shows so the producers thought of me as a TV director. Clint said, "I like Teddy, I've worked with him many times." He sent me the script and I knew we could make a great western picture. And since it was being co-produced by Clint's company, he made sure I got the job.

Post and Eastwood punched up Freeman's script with some ideas of their own, and, according to Post, the director did most of the casting.

> Clint trusted me to find the right people for the roles in the picture. So I relied a lot on people I worked with in television like Pat Hingle, Bruce Dern, Ed Begley, and Charles McGraw, who all knew Clint, having worked with both of us on *Rawhide*. Inger Stevens, the leading lady, had starred on a TV show called *The Farmer's Daughter* and didn't want the part at first because she didn't know Clint's work.

Poster for *Hang 'Em High.*

> But eventually she came around and they became good friends. We
> all did. One day Leonard Freeman, the producer, came on the set
> and started making changes. Well, you don't do that on a picture.
> You can't override the director. So I was about to speak to him and
> Clint stopped me. He said, "Let me do it." Clint goes up to him and
> he says, "If you come on this set again we all walk." He meant it,
> too. We didn't see Lenny again until after we shot the whole picture!

The Oklahoma Territory in 1889 is the setting for the story. Jed Cooper is driving a small herd of cattle across a stream when he is confronted by a posse of nine men. The men are Capt. Wilson (Ed Begley), Reno (Joseph Sirola), Miller (Bruce Dern), Jenkins (Bob Steele), Matt Stone (Alan Hale Jr.), Charlie Blackfoot (Ned Romero), Maddow (Russell Thorson), Tommy (Jonathan Lippe), and Loomis (L. Q. Jones). They surround Cooper and accuse him of cattle rustling. Cooper protests, indicating he has a bill of sale, but apparently the real owner of the cattle was killed and Jed unwittingly did business with his murderer. Accused of murder and cattle rustling, the vigilantes take the law into their own hands, hang Jed Cooper from the limb of a tree, and leave him to die.

While this opening scene, presented before the credits, sets up the story, it also offers substance to the Jed Cooper character. While driving his herd through the creek, Jed notices a calf being swept up by the current. He rescues the calf and gently carries it to the shore while continuing to drive the herd forward. This gentle aspect of the character is far more pronounced than in any of the Leone westerns, and it immediately tells us that Jed Cooper is not Joe, Manco, or Blondie. According to the director:

> That was Clint's idea. He realized an American western needed a
> leading man that was a hero to the audience, and he also knew that
> the script called for him to be a cold blood killer out for vengeance.
> So he came up with that idea so the audience knew right away that
> this was a good guy, an innocent guy.

This was a very clever choice for the character. Jed Cooper is definitely easier to sympathize with—and could be called a hero—while the characters Eastwood played in the Dollars trilogy are intriguing and mysterious, but not particularly heroic.

The next scene features a federal marshal named Dave Bliss seeing Cooper hanging and cutting him down. Cooper is alive, but the wary marshal puts him in irons and takes him to jail in Fort Grant. He is soon released, however, when the territory's judge, Adam Fenton (Pat Hingle) determines he is innocent. Realizing his passion for revenge against those who wrongly hanged him, Fenton makes Cooper a federal marshal, warning him to capture, not kill, the men responsible for the lynching.

One of Eastwood's favorite films was *The Ox Bow Incident* (1943) in which an innocent man is hanged. Ted Post indicated to the author that this film was an inspiration for the plot of *Hang 'Em High*. Its basic premise also exists in the much older horror movie *The Walking Dead* (1936), a Warner Brothers release featuring Boris Karloff as an innocent man who survives electrocution, is pardoned, and goes after the men who frame him, killing them off one by one. This plot was revisited in the low budget *Indestructible Man* (1956) with Lon Chaney Jr. in the title role.

This plot trajectory seems to be followed with the next scene. Cooper sees his saddle on a horse tethered outside a saloon. He goes into the saloon and finds Reno at the bar. Showing the scar on his neck, he intends to take Reno in, but the bandit goes for his gun, and Cooper kills him, much to the judge's chagrin. Word of this incident gets out quickly, so Jenkins turns himself in, reminding Cooper that he had been the lone dissenter among the posse. Cooper remembers and asks the man to provide the names and whereabouts of the others. He does.

During the gun battle between Cooper and Reno, there are edits of close-ups that appear to have been inspired by Leone. Post, however, says they were not.

> You do more close-ups in television because of the small screen. I thought close-ups with Clint, and the intensity of his eyes, would make that scene's confrontation more effective. And you needed a close-up when he lowered the scarf and showed the indentation that the noose left on his neck. My style was a lot different than Leone's. This was an American western and a lot more traditional. I thought Clint was a lot like Gary Cooper—a strong, silent type. Even his name is Cooper in the picture. I don't think that was a coincidence.

Now supplied with the names and whereabouts of the others, Cooper finds Stone working as a blacksmith in the nearby town of Fort Hood. He arrests him, takes him to the sheriff, Ray Calhoun (Charles McGraw), and has him jailed. While it appears to be perhaps the least eventful arrest among the posse, it is quite interesting mostly for the dynamic of the actors. Alan Hale Jr., who plays Stone, had just finished his three-year run as Skipper on the comical TV program *Gilligan's Island*. Clearly inspired by the performance and mannerisms of Oliver Hardy, Hale, who had heretofore usually played tough guys in western films, completely embraced the slapstick silliness of his character on TV, and the popularity of the show made him famous. *Gilligan's Island* went into reruns on weekday afternoons almost immediately on most CBS affiliates; not only was it a recently noted series, but it remained an after-school fixture for children at the time *Hang 'Em High* came out. While clearly typecast in his TV role, director Ted Post did not hesitate to hire Hale for the movie, recalling for the author:

> I knew Alan from other projects, and knew he would be able to register in the part. It was a small one, but an effective one. He was happy to get the part after his TV show was cancelled, but was concerned about the audience reaction. He said to me "people will holler 'hey, there's Skipper' from their theater seats and ruin the scene for the others. I don't want to do that. I don't want to hurt the picture!" I assured him it would be ok, and it turned out just fine.

Hale's command of the role is best proven by Stone's reaction upon seeing a living and breathing Jed Cooper as he is approached. Preoccupied with his duties as a blacksmith, Stone looks up and does what can only be described as a double take. Hale, however, avoids making it look comical, in the manner that Skipper might have done. Instead, his double take registers shock and fear, as if seeing a ghost (and from his immediate perspective, that is pretty close to the truth). He walks, at gunpoint, into the sheriff's office, enters the jail, and puts his head in his hand, facing away from the camera. We do not see his character again.

Sheriff Calhoun, upon seeing the list of persons Marshal Cooper is seeking as part of the posse who hanged him, indicates they are all respected members of the community. Naturally this is unimportant to Cooper. He recruits the sheriff to help him round up the remaining persons, realizing they will consider Calhoun a friendly face and be more open to coming out. On their way, the two of them encounter the survivors of a rustling and murder, and are sidetracked. They catch up with the three men involved, and one turns out to be Miller, part of the posse Cooper is seeking. He is traveling with two brothers, Ben (Richard Gates) and Billy Joe (Bruce Scott). The victims of the rustling want to hang them, but Cooper insists on bringing them back to town alone for trial. He believes the brothers' story that Miller was the murderer and they are only guilty of rustling cattle. Cooper allows them to ride back without being restrained, while Miller remains in handcuffs. "You'll never get me to Fort Grant alive, boy," Miller tells Cooper. "Then I'll get you there dead, boy!" is Cooper's response. Miller attacks Cooper but is overpowered and subdued. The brothers watch, making no attempt to help Miller, despite not being handcuffed.

Ted Post recalled:

> Eastwood and Bruce Dern worked that whole thing out themselves. Bruce was very good at playing the bad guy, and he had worked on *Rawhide*, so they knew and respected each other. It was a good scene, and they both contributed to it equally, Clint even suggesting where to put the camera. Respecting my position, he always asked me if the ideas worked, which they did.

The concept of hanging as the ultimate punishment for crime is a focal point throughout the narrative. Cooper goes on trial and attempts to defend

Bruce Dern and Eastwood.

the two brothers, indicating they made no attempt to help Miller when the two were fighting. The judge points out that they did nothing to help Cooper either. Despite Cooper's best efforts, all three are sent to the gallows. The judge informs him that cattle rustling itself is a hanging offense in Fort Hood, and if they'd been found not guilty, they would be lynched by a mob, while rustlers going unpunished would hamper Oklahoma's bid for statehood. This sequence is also further evidence of the sense of right and wrong that is imbedded in Jed. Despite wanting his vengeance against Miller, he is willing to try and help the other two men, knowing they did not commit a severe offense.

The idea of political factors impeding the swift justice of criminals is a running theme in Eastwood's movie, but in this film it is the attempt to save men from the gallows. The character of Judge Fenton is based on an actual judge by the name of Isaac Parker, known as "the hanging judge," due to his belief that strict law enforcement was the pathway to successful civilization. Character actor Hingle, who would work with Eastwood again, plays the part perfectly; he is able to exhibit a distaste for Cooper's method of doing things, while seeing no problem with his own level of extremism. This more realistic depiction of how justice was dished out in the west is one of the factors that makes this a unique

Hollywood-produced western for its time. There is no clear line between what's right and wrong.

Director Post does a great job with the occasional scenes of public hangings in this movie, as hanging is a recurring theme—be it for justice or vigilante purposes. He presents the large crowds that would attend these "events" even including families with children enjoying a picnic. Former child actress Tammy Locke appeared in these scenes as a seven-year-old, but she still recalls the kindness and support of both Post and Eastwood, telling the author:

> They used to call me a little stinker because I was having a bit too much fun on the set. But I stayed on my mark and knew my lines. Both Eastwood and the director spoke to my mom, who was always on the set, about how impressed they were with me. But my fondest memory is when Clint Eastwood lifted me up to sit with him on that beautiful horse he rode in the movie.

Sheriff Calhoun comes to Fort Grant from Fort Hood and pays Cooper for the cattle he had been driving when confronted by the posse. He accepts the money, indicates he is now even money-wise but will still bring the men to justice for attempted murder. When the sheriff returns to Fort Hood and tells this to the remaining members of the posse, both Blackfoot and Maddow flee but Wilson, Tommy, and Loomis travel to Fort Grant to finish the job on Cooper. While the town is distracted by the spectacle of Miller and the two brothers being hanged, he is ambushed by Wilson, Tommy, and Loomis. He survives the attack and is nursed back to health by Rachel Warren (Inger Stevens) with whom he starts to develop a relationship. Upon his recovery, he leaves to finish his own job of bringing the criminals to justice.

While Inger Stevens reportedly enjoyed her role in this movie and working with Eastwood (and being directed by Ted Post who said, "She gave me a big hug after the picture wrapped and thanked me for casting her"), the romance in the movie is more of a distraction than an organic part of the narrative. It appears to be dropped in to have some level of love interest in the movie, and never really goes anywhere. It is perhaps the only really dull spot in an otherwise very intriguing western.

Cooper returns to Fort Hood and engages in a gunfight with the three men who ambushed him. He kills Tommy and Loomis, but upon cornering Wilson, he bursts in to find that the man has hanged himself, offering a culmination to the film's common theme. The film ends with Cooper riding off to search for the remaining two members of the posse, Blackfoot and Maddow, continuing on his quest for justice that may never end.

Edward Gallafent stated in *Clint Eastwood: Filmmaker and Star*:

When Jed rides out at the end of *Hang 'Em High*, he is not seen as the wandering, pioneering rider who backs a benign, infant civilization and its other, more domestically inclined, men and women. His departure from the town does not have the pathos associated with leaving something of value, or being rejected by it, or some combination of these things. Jed rides past the gallows, down the main street, and out of town. A positive statement might have been implied by having Rachel, or even the judge, watch him depart. But no one pays any attention whatsoever.

Ted Post offers a visually stunning film, utilizing not only the close-ups he had mastered as a TV director, but understanding how the expanse of the wide-screen image would be particularly effective for establishing shots. There is always a tension, an unsettling air to the proceedings, with the concerns of the criminals, of Cooper's need for justice, and of the judge's strict law enforcement coupled with his political aspirations and misgivings about his new marshal's methods. Post directs a strong cast of veteran actors to offer some of their best work. One of the most interesting shots in the movie occurs during the hanging sequence as Post is panning the crowd and showing the huge mass of people who have come out to witness this spectacle. The camera shows a bunch of feet dangling, which appear to be hanged men, until the camera pans back to reveal they are merely spectators.

Eastwood received $400,000 for this movie, along with 25 percent of the gross. Along with acting and producing (which included some level of supervision at nearly every level of production), Eastwood also performed his own stunt work, including being dragged by a horse with a rope around his neck at the outset of the film. His taking his work so seriously while acting as his own producer for the first time was something of a portent to what he would quickly become. As his career rapidly progressed, Eastwood would just as rapidly rise as a filmmaker whose work was consistently well produced.

Hang 'Em High was a major success, and it was the biggest box office opening for United Artists in its history, with an opening day revenue of $5,241 in Baltimore alone. It debuted at number five on *Variety*'s weekly survey of top films and had made its money back within two weeks of screening. According to Patrick McGilligan, Arthur Winsten of the *New York Post* called it "A Western of quality, courage, danger and excitement." Roger Ebert in the *Chicago Sun Times* stated:

> Eastwood has made the big time, and Hollywood has brought him back home to star in *Hang 'em High*. As was the case with the Italian Westerns, *Hang 'em High* is a revenge story. The moral of the story is vaguely against capital punishment.

From its shocking opening to its effectively ambiguous conclusion, *Hang 'Em High* is nearly as great and progressive an American western as the Dollars trilogy had been Italian ones. Its box office success ensured Eastwood's further success with his own production company, and rather than pigeon-hole himself into a recurring character, he decided to explore what else he could do with the western hero. With his next film, Eastwood decided to take the rudiments of the conventional movie cowboy and place him in the crowded big city. While hardly an original idea, Eastwood's approach further informed his understanding of how much the western genre could be expanded.

Note

1. Originally designed to help independent filmmakers, Malpaso soon became a top-level production company.

CHAPTER 6

Coogan's Bluff (1968)

(A Universal-Malpaso Company Picture)
Director: Don Siegel
Screenplay: Herman Miller, Dean Riesner, Howard Rodman
Story: Herman Miller
Producer: Don Siegel
Associate Producer: Irving L. Leonard
Executive Producer: Richard E. Lyons
Music: Lalo Schifrin
Cinematography: Bud Thackery, Robert Surtees
Editing: Sam E. Waxman
Cast: Clint Eastwood (Coogan); Lee J. Cobb (Lt. McElroy); Susan Clark (Julie Roth); Tisha Sterling (Linny Raven); Don Stroud (James Ringerman); Betty Field (Ellen Ringerman); Tom Tully (Sheriff McCrea); Melodie Johnson (Millie); James Edwards (Sgt. Jackson); Rudy Diaz (Running Bear); David Doyle (Pushie); Louis Zorich (Taxi Driver); Meg Myles (Big Red); Skip Battyn (Omega); Marjorie Bennett (Mrs. Fowler); Seymour Cassel (Young Hood); John Coe (Bellboy); Albert Popwell (Wonderful Digby); Conrad Bain (Madison Avenue Man); Larry Duran (Zig Zag); James Gavin (Ferguson); Jerry Summers (Good Eyes); Antonia Rey (Mrs. Amador); Scott Hale (Dr. Scott); Allen Pinson (Whippy); Albert Henderson (Desk Sergeant); James McCallion (Room Clerk); Syl Lamont (Manager), Jess Osuna, Doug Reid (Prison Hospital Guards); Marya Henriques (Go-Go Dancer); Eve Brent (Hooker); David Brandon, Linda Clifford, Colleen Thornton, Morreen Thornton (Hippies); Constance Davis (Mother); George Fargo, Diki Lerner (Gay Boys); James Joyce (Man at Pigeon-Toed Orange Peel); Ted Jacques, Al Ruban (Detectives); Clark Warren (Plainclothesman); Kathleen O'Malley (Woman); Robert Osterloh (Deputy); Clifford A. Pellow (Deputy); Diana Rose (Psychedelic Paint Girl); Don Siegel, Kristoffer Tabori (Elevator Passengers); James Oliver, James McEachin (Bits).
Budget: $3,000,000
Gross: $3,110,000

Release Date: October 2, 1968
Running Time: 93 minutes
Sound Mix: Mono (Westrex Recording System)
Color: Technicolor
Aspect Ratio: 1.85: 1
Available on DVD from Universal

Director Don Siegel seemed to gravitate toward stories about a central figure attempting to cope within limited parameters, being forced to adapt to methods that go against what he has always understood to be the best and most effective. His vision was best explored in his films with Clint Eastwood, and their first collaboration is *Coogan's Bluff.* They would work together several more times, including on the iconic *Dirty Harry* (1971) a few years later.

Eastwood, wanting to expand his character, was attracted to this story of a modern-day Arizona lawman who maintained the perspective of a westerner even after being placed in New York City, where his pursuit of a criminal is beset with liberal sensibilities beyond his scope of understanding. While Eastwood himself is often labeled a Republican, he always labeled himself a social liberal and a fiscal conservative. He supported abortion rights and gay marriage and was against U.S. involvement in the Vietnam War. Siegel was a straight-ahead liberal. But the context of the film, putting Eastwood's character among progressive-type characters that seemed unsettling to a lot of middle America as far back as the late 1960s, was a good way to elicit not only a deeper understanding of the character, but the potential for some humorous scenes. *Coogan's Bluff* is not the cinematic equivalent of *The Good, the Bad, and the Ugly* (1966), but it is among the most entertaining of the earlier Eastwood productions. Perhaps it can be argued that *Coogan's Bluff* is not a western in the strictest sense, but the idea of taking Eastwood's western lawman character from the plains and placing him into a modern setting makes this film a necessary part of our study.

Deputy sheriff Walt Coogan (Eastwood) travels from his native Arizona to New York City to extradite a prisoner, James Ringerman (Don Stroud). When he gets there, he is met by Detective Lieutenant McElroy (Lee J. Cobb), who indicates that Ringerman cannot be moved until he recovers from an LSD overdose. Furthermore, Coogan is told he must obtain extradition papers from the Supreme Court of New York State in order to proceed.

The film's opening scene presents it as a modern-day western. A drifter in the Arizona desert is perched on a mountain awaiting the lawman, who approaches not on a horse, but in a truck. A gunfight ensues, and the man is eventually caught and brought to jail. This is a standard situation for a western

Eastwood in *Coogan's Bluff*.

movie, but the vehicle Eastwood drives to pursue the criminal indicates it is taking place in a contemporary setting.

Looking awkward and out of place in his imposing cowboy hat, Coogan is an obvious outsider immediately upon arriving in New York. In a city that defines diversity, he presents an image that nets double takes and stares. However, the film quickly informs us that while he may be an old-school western anachronism, he is also nobody's fool. When a cab driver charges him "$2.95 including the luggage," Coogan asks: "How many Bloomingdales in New York?"

> Cabdriver: Just one.
>
> Coogan: We passed it twice.
>
> Cabdriver: $2.95 including the luggage!
>
> Coogan: Here's three dollars, including the tip.

While Coogan is immediately pegged as a rube by the cabdriver, he has the wiles to avoid being duped. He may not be a perfect fit for this faster-paced urban society, but his rural background does not limit his intelligence or effectiveness.

The same reaction occurs when Coogan meets Lieutenant McElroy, who is the quintessential gruff New York detective that had already become a staple as far back as narrative cinema. He is skeptical of this outsider, and as he runs down the litany of obstacles that define the area's due process, Coogan wonders why he cannot simply grab the prisoner by the scruff of his neck and haul him back to Arizona.

Another more revealing relationship occurs when Coogan meets social worker Julie (Susan Clark). While she is speaking to a client, the client brazenly puts his hand on her breast. She asks him not to, but not in an angry or frightened manner. She appears to accept this behavior as a sort of disability and merely attempts to redirect him. Coogan sees this and slaps the man away. For doing so, he is reprimanded by the social worker. Confused, Coogan attempts to apologize to her, but he refuses to apologize to the client. The social worker eventually cools off and accepts a dinner invitation from Coogan, as she represents the girlfriend of the man he is to extradite. When she attempts to pay the check, Coogan reminds her that she is a woman and "should act like it." Feminism is a foreign concept to Coogan, as it would have been to much of middle America (especially middle-aged America). The film would continue to present aspects of the slowly growing counterculture as confusion to Coogan.

Coogan himself is hardly a man of pure scruples. He uses the social worker to obtain information about her client, which allows him to go to where he is being held, bluff the attendants into turning him over, and proceed to take him back to Arizona. He is ambushed by Ringerman's girlfriend, Linny (Tisha Sterling), and tavern owner Pushie (David Doyle), allowing the prisoner to escape. Coogan continues to use Julie; he secures an invitation to her house and finds out Linny's name and address by quietly searching the files in her home office.

He attempts to use Linny in the same manner. She brings him to a pool room where he is attacked by Pushie and several other men. Coogan puts up a good fight but is eventually overpowered. He manages to kill Pushie and some others before the men scatter upon hearing sirens. Lieutenant McElroy arrives to find the pool room in a shambles, with Coogan's cowboy hat on the floor.

Coogan's methods are strategic and appear to be an attempt to cut through the red tape of due process that has been thrown before him as an obstacle. Julie is chagrined at being used, but she continues to be smitten by the tall, imposing lawman—mostly because he is so unlike any man she has encountered. He seems very courtly and confident, which she finds attractive, even as she realizes he is using her for his own gain. McElroy is the typical harried detective who responds with exasperation toward the western lawman's methods. This dynamic would be utilized to even greater impact in the eventual Dirty Harry series. This film is an interesting contrast to the previous *Hang 'Em High* (1968). Rather than being given free rein to exact justice, Coogan is restricted from utilizing his methods of tracking down the criminal.

When Coogan finally meets up with Linny again, his old-fashioned western methods eschew all level of manners. He gets quite rough with the young lady, threatening her life if she does not reveal Ringerman's whereabouts. This leads to a motorcycle chase through New York streets with Ringerman finally apprehended.

Ending a police drama with a chase sequence had become in vogue around this time, the best examples being *Bullit* (1968) and, later, *The French Connection* (1971). It is nicely shot in *Coogan's Bluff*, the editing and tracking shots building up consistent excitement. But the film calms down in the final shots, with Coogan handcuffed to Ringerman on a plane back to Arizona. Coogan takes out a cigarette and lights it. He then offers one to the handcuffed prisoner,

Eastwood and Tisha Sterling.

putting it in his mouth and lighting it for him. In the classic tradition of the western film, lawman and criminal have a begrudging respect for one another. Julie is then shown below, waving good-bye during the takeoff. Despite his being an outsider, Coogan has achieved success and made an impact.

While one can argue that elements of the narrative and characters have dated, *Coogan's Bluff* is actually a fascinating depiction of how cinema presented areas of the counterculture. Hippies, gay people, and drug users are all presented in rather garish stereotypes, indicating these new trends were not only confusing but could be dangerous. At the time, such an attitude might alienate younger moviegoers, but that does not appear to be the demographic this film is trying to reach. It should be noted that progressive ideas are not challenged, only bureaucratic red tape, and such superficial things as hairstyles and fashions, the latter usually done for humorous purposes. Coogan has a wry sense of sarcasm with much of his dialogue. At one point, Julie states, "I only handle single young girls," and Coogan replies, "Yeah, me, too." It is also worth noting that this aspect of a person being out of place in an environment isn't played for comedy, as in so many other films. While the film does have many amusing moments, overall it is still much more of a drama than a comedy.

But is it a western? Not in the conventional sense. Coogan is an Arizona lawman who, for all intents and purposes, is a cowboy of the modern era as well as the film's central figure. He drives an automobile rather than riding a horse in the opening scene described at the beginning of this chapter, but he remains a man whose ways and mores are steeped in western tradition. With this assignment, he must respond to changing behavioral modes within the trappings of a big city, where his rustic background is challenged on a most basic level. Thus, *Coogan's Bluff* examines the western hero from another perspective. Coogan is a rustic man from another place, but he is smart enough to avoid being taken by the cabdriver. He can still operate a motorcycle as effectively as his immediate ancestors would have given chase on horseback.

The late 1960s was a time of many challenges within pop culture's tradition. *Coogan's Bluff* challenges the western in a far different manner than Leone's films had. While the Leone movies were westerns that defied convention, *Coogan's Bluff* features the conventional western stereotype in a big city police drama. That both director and star would explore that further with *Dirty Harry* makes this film even more significant to our study.

The preparation of this movie is nearly as entertaining as the film itself. The original script was penned by Herman Miller and Jack Laird, whose work Eastwood had known from teleplays they had written for *Rawhide*. Once Don Siegel came on the project, several rewrites occurred. When the updated screenplay was delivered to Eastwood after a reported seven rewrites, he called a meeting and indicated he hated it, insisting on going back to the original writers' idea. Siegel and Eastwood laid out all seven drafts of the script on the floor of the director's office, picking out sequences that they liked from each. They then hired writer Dean Riesner to put it together into something of coherence. Although he worked quickly, the script still had not been completed once filming commenced. Despite all of this, the movie's narrative was clear, and its points were made. This was Clint Eastwood's first movie for Universal since his early days under contract in the 1950s doing small roles. As a sort of inside joke, when Coogan enters a New York club, the television in the background is playing the film *Tarantula*, in which Eastwood had appeared earlier in his career. Now, a dozen years later, Eastwood was a leading man, ran his own production company, and commanded a million-dollar salary for *Coogan's Bluff.*

At the time of its release, much was made about the violent subject matter. The Motion Picture Association of America (MPAA) ratings system was not established until November 1968, around a month after *Coogan's Bluff* was released. Some newspapers would indicate when films were suggested for mature audiences, but there were no ratings as of yet when this movie came out. Thus, more realistic presentations of violence and brutality were just beginning to find their way into American movies, matching what had already been going on in Europe (as the Leone films indicate).

Eastwood was successfully carving a niche for himself while reinventing the movie tough guy persona with his own style. Vincent Canby in the *New York Times* stated:

> If James Dean had lived to grow a few inches taller and to attain a lean, graceful, movie middle-age (anything from his late 20's to his 60's), and if he had been tranquilized beyond all emotion, the result would have been Clint Eastwood, one of the movie phenomena of today. Like some of the most popular movie stars of the past (Alan Ladd, for example), Eastwood doesn't act in motion pictures; he is framed in them. In *Coogan's Bluff,* the contemporary melodrama that opened yesterday, Eastwood plays an Arizona sheriff (Coogan), a sort of "Cactus Jim" Bond, who comes to New York to extradite a local hood for trial back home. In a world of shabby precinct stations, posh apartments, strobe-lighted discothèques and Hollywood-style New York hippies, Eastwood becomes an unconscious parody of himself and, for that matter, of all movie superheroes. He moves through it all talking in low monosyllables, getting beaten to a pulp (without lasting effect) and turning women on and off like light switches, according to the conventions of the genre. The mythic hero of Leone's West looks as out of place in Manhattan as Tarzan might, since he is constantly being upstaged by more colorful minor characters and the restless scenery of the big city.

It is notable how this review dismisses Eastwood's economy of movement as "being tranquilized beyond all emotion" and stating that Eastwood does not act in movies but "is merely framed in them," comparing him to Alan Ladd. Ladd, who scored brilliantly in the film noir *This Gun for Hire* (1942) and as the title character in the classic western *Shane* (1953), has gone down in history as one of the most effective actors of his time. So has Clint Eastwood.

For his next project, Eastwood agreed to take a role in a major screen version of a stage musical with a western theme. His character would be far closer to Rowdy Yates than any of those he'd played in his more recent westerns. It was a curious choice, and not a particularly good one.

CHAPTER 7

Paint Your Wagon (1969)

(An Alan Jay Lerner production for the Malpaso Company; released by Paramount Pictures)

Director: Joshua Logan
Screenplay, Book, and Lyrics: Alan Jay Lerner
Adaptation: Paddy Chayefsky
Producer: Alan Jay Lerner
Cinematography: William A. Fraker
Editing: Robert C. Jones
Cast: Lee Marvin (Ben Rumson); Clint Eastwood (Pardner); Jean Seberg (Elizabeth); Harve Presnell (Rotten Luck Willie); Ray Walston (Mad Jack Duncan); Tom Ligon (Horton Fenty); Alan Dexter (Parson); William O'Connell (Horace Tabor); Benny Baker (Haywood Holbrook); Alan Baxter (Mr. Fenty); Paula Trueman (Mrs. Fenty); Robert Easton (Atwell); Geoffrey Norman (Foster); H. B. Haggerty (Steve Bull); Terry Jenkins (Joe Mooney); Karl Bruck (Schermerhorn); John Mitchum (Jacob Woodling); Sue Casey (Sarah Woodling); Eddie Little Sky (Indian); Harvey Parry (Higgins); H. W. Gim (Wong); William Mims (Frock-coated Man); Dolores Domasin (Princess Hummingbird); Roy Jenson (Hennessey); Pat Hawley (Clendennon); Amber Flower (Laura Sue Fenty); Daniel Keough (Pioneer); Harry Lauter (Peddler); Patricia Smith (Dance Hall Girl); Jerry Whittington (Prospector); Tony Giorgio (Card Player); Ralph Barr, Jimmie Fadden, Jeff Hanna, Chris Darrow, John McEuen (Nitty Gritty Dirt Band); Gabrielle Rossillon, Michele Montau, Marina Maubert, Barbara Gabrielle, Rena Horten, Danielle Cotet (French Bawds); Lisa Todd (American Bawd); Richard Farnsworth, John McKee, Wayne McLaren, Michael Donovan O'Donnell, Frank Orsatti, Murray Staff, Edward Rickard, John Hudkins, Leroy Johnson, Larry Martinelli, Tony Epper, Cal Barlett, Joe Brooks, Boyd Cabeen, Tony Colti, Henry A. Escalante, George Fargo, Lee Faulkner, Paul Harper, Jay S. York, Jack Williams, Dar Robinson, Victor Romito, Walt La Rue, Nick Klar, David Sharpe, Joe Yrigoyen, Buddy Van Horn, Fred Waugh, Jerome Sheldon, Walt Davis (Miners).

Soundtrack:

"I'm on My Way" (music by Frederick Loewe; lyrics by Alan Jay Lerner). Sung by the Chorus.

"I Still See Elisa" (music by Frederick Loewe; lyrics by Alan Jay Lerner). Sung by Clint Eastwood.

"The First Thing You Know" (music by André Previn; lyrics by Alan Jay Lerner). Sung by Lee Marvin.

"Hand Me Down That Can of Beans" (music by Frederick Loewe; lyrics by Alan Jay Lerner). Sung by the Nitty Gritty Dirt Band and the Chorus.

"They Call the Wind Maria" (music by Frederick Loewe; lyrics by Alan Jay Lerner). Sung by Harve Presnell and the Chorus.

"Whoop-Ti-Ay! (Shivaree)" (music by Frederick Loewe; lyrics by Alan Jay Ler-ner). Sung by the Chorus.

"A Million Miles Away behind the Door" (music by André Previn; lyrics by Alan Jay Lerner). Sung by Anita Gordon; dubbing by Jean Seberg.

"I Talk to the Trees" (music by Frederick Loewe; lyrics by Alan Jay Lerner). Sung by Clint Eastwood.

"There's a Coach Comin' In" (music by Frederick Loewe; lyrics by Alan Jay Lerner). Sung by Harve Presnell and the Chorus.

"The Gospel of No Name City" (music by André Previn; lyrics by Alan Jay Lerner). Sung by Alan Dexter.

"Best Things" (music by André Previn; lyrics by Alan Jay Lerner). Sung by Lee Marvin, Ray Walston, and Clint Eastwood.

"Wand'rin' Star" (music by Frederick Loewe; lyrics by Alan Jay Lerner). Sung by Lee Marvin and the Chorus.

"Gold Fever" (music by André Previn; lyrics by Alan Jay Lerner). Sung by Clint Eastwood and the Chorus.

Finale ("I'm on My Way"). Sung by Lee Marvin, Ray Walston, and the Chorus.

Budget: $20,000,000 (estimated)

Gross: $31,678,778 (USA)

Release Date: October 15, 1969

Running Time: 158 minutes

Sound Mix: 4-Track Stereo (35 mm prints); 6-Track (70 mm prints)

Color: Technicolor

Aspect Ratio: 2.35: 1

Availability: DVD (Paramount Home Video)

Clint Eastwood chose his next project because he liked the script and because it gave him a chance to sing—a talent he had that was never utilized. *Paint Your Wagon* was a stage musical by Alan J. Lerner and Fritz Loewe, the creators of *My Fair Lady* and *Camelot*, and it holds the distinction as being one of their least successful Broadway productions. When plans were made to film it, the Pulitzer Prize–winning Joshua Logan, who had directed the classic film version of the musical *South Pacific*, was hired to direct, while writer Paddy Chayefsky was hired to write the screenplay. According to Richard Schickel in his biography of Eastwood:

> Chayefsky's work bore no resemblance to the book Lerner had written for the 1951 Broadway production, which recounted the adventures of a widower and his daughter searching for new lives, new wealth (and in her case a new love) in a California mining camp during the Gold Rush era. The playwright retained the setting of the original show, and fond a place for most of its songs (plus some new ones that Lerner wrote with Andre Previn) but threw out everything else.

Chayefsky had changed the story line, and the result was a dark, moody theme that was a lot different than the usual upbeat musicals. In the late 1960s, the musical was falling quickly out of vogue, and fewer were being produced. They cost a lot to make, and for every hit like *Mary Poppins* or *The Sound of Music* there were bombs like *Star!*

When Clint Eastwood saw Chayefsky's script, he felt this darker, more offbeat approach could redefine and ultimately resurrect the movie musical in the same manner as Sergio Leone's films had done for the western genre. Lee Marvin turned down a role in Sam Peckinpah's *The Wild Bunch* (1969) in order to take the lead in this film for a million-dollar fee, while Eastwood was hired for $750,000.

Eastwood went off to film *Where Eagles Dare* (1968) after signing on to do *Paint Your Wagon.* Unfortunately, several rewrites later, the film evolved into the sort of lightweight musical fluff that Eastwood had no interest in doing. He had an escape clause in his contract, so he could leave the project if he did not approve of the script. According to Schickel, Eastwood stated:

> I get this thing, and I start reading it, and now it's totally different. It has no relation to the original, except the names of the characters. They had the threesome deal, but it wasn't a dark story at all. It was all fluffy. Fluffy and running around talking, and they're having Lee do *Cat Ballou II.*

Schickel also wrote that Paddy Chayefsky indicated only six pages of his script remained in the final version. His writing credit was demoted to "adapted by" in the credits. Lerner and Loewe told Eastwood that musicals had to be upbeat. At first he instructed his management to get him out of his contract, but eventually he decided to play the role, not wanting to garner a reputation at being difficult. According to Schickel, Eastwood decided to do as he did in *Rawhide* and try to make it interesting.

Clint Eastwood plays a farmer who is found near death by a prospector. The two discover gold in the California gold country; they form a partnership, with Eastwood simply known as Pardner, while Marvin plays Ben Rumson. Once the discovery becomes known, No Name City, as it is called, becomes the habitat of miners from all over. It is an all-male town, and their longing for some female companionship is further emphasized when a Mormon with two wives comes to camp. Believing his having two wives to their none is unfair, arrangements are made for him to sell one of the wives to the highest bidder. One wife, Elizabeth,

Eastwood and Lee Marvin in *Paint Your Wagon*.

is so unhappy with her current circumstances that she volunteers to be the wife sold. Ben becomes the highest bidder and marries Elizabeth, who, on their wedding night, states, "I hope I will make a good wife." Ben rips the front of her dress, sees her ample bosom, and states, "You sure as hell will," while hastily undressing himself. She pulls a gun on him and demands to be treated with respect.

From this point, and throughout the duration of the movie, musical numbers are interspersed among scenes of drinking, gambling, prostitution, wife sharing, and a bit of gold mining. There are some mildly amusing moments as Ben is domesticated against his will, building a home for his wife with the help of other miners, and becoming jealous when he believes all the others are smitten by her. Plans are made to kidnap six French prostitutes who are set to arrive at a nearby town, the men believing that prostitution can net more money for No Name City from visiting miners. Meanwhile, Elizabeth becomes interested in Pardner, while also having affection for Ben. Her Mormon reasoning is that if a man can have two wives, a woman can have two husbands. The film concludes with the discovery of gold dust in the floorboards of the saloons in No Name City. They tunnel under the buildings, weakening the foundations, and cause the entire town to collapse.

The results were aesthetically unrewarding. One song, "They Call the Wind Maria," was quite good as evident by various pop recordings over the years, but otherwise the soundtrack is forgettable (although it should be noted that "Wand'rin' Star" was a hit in the UK). The talent involved does its best, and there are a few amusing moments; however, as Clint Eastwood's western films go, *Paint Your Wagon* is certainly the weakest. When *Paint Your Wagon* was released, Roger Ebert stated:

> *Paint Your Wagon* doesn't inspire a review. It doesn't even inspire a put-down. It just lies there in my mind—a big, heavy lump. But in the midst of it, like a visitor from another movie, Lee Marvin desperately labors to inject some flash and sparkle. And he succeeds in bringing whole scenes to life. A good actor can do this, but it's a waste when he must. The problem was money. It always is in these inflated big-budget musicals. The curse of overproduction even destroys the small, private scenes. Clint Eastwood wanders through the forest, singing (or, more accurately, whining) "I Talk to the Trees." And suddenly there's what sounds like the Red Army Chorus, booming in the background. The result is loud and officially stereophonic, all right. But it's studio music—cold, aloof, manufactured. There's no feeling that this might be a guy in the forest, singing a song. OK, maybe it was time to break away from the sloppy sentimentality of most musicals. But *Paint Your Wagon* doesn't. Most of the time, it's simultaneously suggestive and puritanical—so we snicker but we don't laugh.

Other reviews were no better. Charles Champlin of the *Los Angeles Times* called the film "coarse and unattractive" but singled out Eastwood for praise, stating that his "stoic and handsome dignity stands out and he sings in an unscholarly baritone that is fine." *Newsweek* stated, "Rarely has a film wasted so much time so wantonly."

The budget for this movie was originally $10 million, but the final amount was double that. It cost $80,000 per day to transport the cast and crew to the filming location, the closest hotel being over fifty miles away. The set used for the mining camp cost $2.4 million to build. Also Lee Marvin was drinking quite heavily during most of the shooting, resulting in a lot of retakes. The only positive aspect of this experience was Clint Eastwood's frustration with the constant delays in making this movie, which more firmly convinced him to be his own director.

Despite all of its troubles, *Paint Your Wagon* was Paramount's sixth largest success up to that point, along with being one of the top ten highest grossing films of 1969. It may have shown there was an audience for a musical that ran three hours and featured top stars in a bloated production, but it did nothing to advance Clint Eastwood's career.

But is it a western? It can be argued that *Paint Your Wagon* is a musical and is thus no more a part of the western genre than, say, *Blazing Saddles* (1974). In fact, in a comprehensive study of an actor-filmmaker's westerns, it is necessary to include offshoots that fall within the western genre despite some uncharacteristic elements. *Paint Your Wagon* is one of those movies.

CHAPTER 8

Two Mules for Sister Sara (1970)

(A Universal-Malpaso Company Picture in association with Sanen Productions)

Director: Don Siegel
Screenplay: Albert Maltz
Story: Budd Boetticher
Producers: Carroll Case, Martin Rackin
Music: Ennio Morricone
Cinematography: Gabriel Figueroa, Robert Surtees
Editing: Robert F. Shugrue
Cast: Shirley MacLaine (Sara); Clint Eastwood (Hogan); Manolo Fábregas (Colonel Beltran); Alberto Morin (General LeClaire); Armando Silvestre (1st American); John Kelly (2nd American); Enrique Lucero (3rd American); David Estuardo (Juan); Ada Carrasco (Juan's Mother); Pancho Córdova (Juan's Father); José Chávez (Horatio); Pedro Galván, José Ángel Espinosa, Aurora Muñoz, Xavier Marc, Hortensia Santoveña, Rosa Furman, José Torvay, Margarito Luna (Bits).
Budget: $4,000,000
Gross: $4,700,000
Release Date: June 16, 1970
Running Time: 116 minutes
Sound Mix: Mono (Westrex Recording System)
Color: Technicolor
Aspect Ratio: 2.35: 1
Availability: DVD and Blu-ray (Universal)

At this point in his career, Clint Eastwood was in transition. Now once again making films for Universal after having been under contract with this studio as an overlooked, small-time actor a decade earlier, Eastwood fluctuated between his own projects and those he was cast in by the studio. While *Hang 'Em High* (1968) and *Coogan's Bluff* (1968) afforded him some creative input, being cast in movies like *Where Eagles Dare* (1968) and *Kelly's Heroes* (1970) did little or nothing to advance his career.

While he was filming *Where Eagles Dare*, Clint Eastwood was contacted by Elizabeth Taylor with a script that producer Martin Rackin planned to do at Universal. The screenplay was by Budd Boetticher, known as the director of such top-drawer Randolph Scott films as *Seven Men from Now* (1956) and *Buchanan Rides Alone* (1958). Eastwood was attracted to the project after reading an early draft of the script, and he agreed to co-star with Taylor. Eastwood gave the script to Don Siegel, who expressed an interest in directing. What Eastwood did not realize was that when Boetticher sold his story to Rackin, he was under the impression that he'd be allowed to direct. Rackin, a producer whom Richard Schickel described as "all gold chains, sunlamp tan, and tough talk," fired Boetticher from the project and hired Albert Maltz to write the screenplay. Maltz, a member of the infamous Hollywood Ten, who had been imprisoned and blacklisted during the McCarthy era, would be getting a writing credit on a movie for the first time in over twenty years. Rackin also took Elizabeth Taylor off the project, with no explanation to Eastwood or Siegel, and hired Shirley MacLaine as the leading lady. The script, as originally written, featured a Hispanic character as the central female figure, which Taylor could have pulled off, but certainly not the fair-skinned, red-headed MacLaine. That portion of the story was reworked. While Boetticher retained a story credit on the released film, he was not consulted throughout the process.

This is understandable. The perspective that the producer wanted was to extend from the character Eastwood had now established with the moviegoing public via the Leone westerns, as Eastwood and Ted Post had done with *Hang 'Em High*. Boetticher represented the classic American western, and while he was responsible for helming some of the finest classics in this genre, he did not like the sarcasm, the cynicism, or the ultra violence of Leone's redefinition of the western film (many classic western filmmakers and actors felt the same, including John Wayne). Despite the frivolity of his external appearance and manner, producer Rackin had the right idea to fashion the script more akin to what made Eastwood successful, and to use Don Siegel as director. *Two Mules for Sister Sara* is, like *Coogan's Bluff*, an example of solid, entertaining cinema.

As with Eastwood's previous westerns, everything is established and defined in the opening scene. Hogan, a drifter (Eastwood) sees a woman (Shirley MacLaine) with her clothing ripped away, about to be raped by three men. He fires

Poster for *Two Mules for Sister Sara*.

a shot to stop them, and they respond by inviting him to join in the festivities, even indicating that they have whiskey. Shots are fired, and one of them grabs the woman as a human shield. Hogan, remaining at a distance, is shown sitting against a rock, seemingly ignoring the man as he lights a cigar. He then pulls out a stick of dynamite, casually lights it with his cigar, and tosses it toward the man, who lets go of the woman and runs away. Hogan shoots the man in the back, walks at an even pace to the dynamite, and removes the fuse.

As with the jarring opening of *Hang 'Em High*, the first scene depicts violence against the innocent. And like his initial appearance in *A Fistful of Dollars*, Eastwood's opening scene finds him spying trouble where a woman is involved. Finally, in the same consistent manner as most of Don Siegel's films, *Two Mules for Sister Sara* deals with the attempt to adapt to people and surroundings outside of the central character's comfort zone. In this movie, there are two central characters.

Siegel's filming of the opening scene is a part of why it works so well. He never lets us get any closer to the action than Hogan's vantage point, only eliminating the distance after the first shot is fired. Once one of the men grabs the woman, daring Hogan to fire again, Siegel cuts to a medium profile shot of the drifter sitting majestically against the rock, lighting a cigar with complete aplomb, confusing the gunman (Siegel quickly cutting away to that reaction). Once he pulls out the stick of dynamite and casually lights it with the cigar, we realize his method of defense. The panicked gunman flees. The fact that Hogan shoots him in the back is likely something a director like Boetticher would not allow, but Eastwood had already broken that unwritten code of western movies in previous films. It is a particularly powerful opening and sets the tone for the remainder of the movie.

> The woman: They told me they were going to kill me!
>
> Hogan: Well, they aren't telling you much now, are they?

The woman is Sara, a nun connected with helping Mexican revolutionaries in their battle against the French. Coincidentally (and perhaps a bit conveniently), Hogan has arranged to assist the Mexican attack the French garrison with the promise of some of the strongbox's contents if they're successful. Hogan accompanies Sara to the Mexican camp.

Hogan must curb his behavior around the nun, with some similarities to the dynamic between Katharine Hepburn and Humphrey Bogart in *The African Queen* (1951) or perhaps Hepburn and John Wayne in *Rooster Cogburn (and the Lady)* (1979). This fits in with director Siegel's theme of having to adapt to immediate circumstances outside of one's comfort zone. It also exhibits an unlikely partnership, something Siegel would also revisit, as would Eastwood, in subsequent movies. Initially, Sara is submissive toward Hogan, who assumes his role as the alpha male leader. Almost immediately, he expresses sexual frustration:

> Hogan: You shouldn't be so good looking.
>
> Sara: I am married to the Lord.
>
> Hogan: Yeah, that's what I'm steamed about.

Sexual tension is discernible throughout the duo's relationship during the movie's opening scenes. At regular intervals, the nun reveals more and more about herself to the puzzled drifter. She smokes his cigars, drinks his whiskey, and refers to her buttocks as an ass. When he asks where she heard such language, she claims a fellow nun taught it to her. "I'd sure like to know what she did before she became a nun," is Hogan's bemused response.

Many of the early scenes center upon the gentle earnestness of Sara and the macho command of Hogan. Hogan must kill a rattlesnake that is discovered during a place where they are to camp for the night. Walking slowly through the tall grass, Hogan listens for the rattle of the snake. As it lurches out, he steps on it and cuts off its head. Handing the headless snake to Sara, he states, "If we get split up this will make good eatin'."

In his biography, *A Siegel Film*, Don Siegel recalled:

> I decided to shoot a reverse on Shirley reacting to the coiling of the
> snake; Clint sticking the bottom of his boot towards the striking
> snake; Clint's foot stamping down just behind its head and his knife
> cutting off its head. The last thing I wanted to shoot was the actual
> snake, as we only had one. When I rehearsed with Shirley, her reac-
> tions were unbelievably unconcerned. I explained that she must show
> fear, revulsion, actually recoiling from what she is presumably seeing.
>
> MacLaine: I've killed rattlesnakes in my backyard. It's no big deal.
> Certainly it's nothing to be frightened of.
>
> Me: But Shirley, in the part you're playing in the picture, you are
> frightened. Clint is the hero. In your eyes, what he is doing is ex-
> tremely dangerous.
>
> MacLaine: Well, it isn't.
>
> Me: Whether it is, or not, your character must think it is. So please,
> let's get on with it. I must have strong reactions to the killing of the
> rattlesnake.
>
> I presume she tried; but I was not pleased with her performance.
> However, when I showed Clint's encounter with the rattlesnake, I
> heard her gasp, "Must we kill it?" Unfortunately, her magnificent
> reaction was off scene. When Clint cut the head of the rattlesnake off,
> he stood up and handed it to her. Her face was green. She was shak-
> ing with fear and revulsion. I uttered a crisp command, "Don't drop
> it!" Trembling, she held on to the snake, which was still squirming. I
> yelled, "Cut!" before she had a chance to faint. . . . Clint exited, fast.
> Although Shirley turned greener, she had the guts to hang on to the
> headless, squirming rattlesnake.

Eastwood actually did kill the rattlesnake for the scene, after arguing that he is
opposed to killing animals. Mexican authorities did not want it released in the
area.

In one of the film's most tense and effective scenes, Hogan is shot with an
arrow in the shoulder as he attempts to destroy a French train carrying ammunition. As the poison from the arrowhead seeps into his body, Sara must remove
it while Hogan dazedly gives her instructions. It is a beautifully shot scene,
with Siegel keeping the camera very close to both actors, leaving little room for
negative space. These tight shots add to the tension as Sara carefully follows Hogan's instructions and is able to successfully remove the arrow and bandage the
wound. Hogan alternates between talking and singing to take his mind off the

Don Siegel directing Eastwood.

pain. The nun, completely out of her element, proves to be a good listener who is able to carry out instructions effectively. The injury keeps Hogan from being able to aim his rifle properly to detonate the bomb that will destroy the train, so Sara assists him. This scene is also important to developing the relationship between the characters, as hereafter they both have greater respect for each other.

In a delightful surprise within the context of the narrative, the two make it to the Mexican camp, and Sara leads Hogan to a house where she stays. Hogan is initially shocked, indicating, "Sister Sara, this is a cat house," whereupon Sara replies, "No, Hogan, this is a whore house," revealing that she is not a nun, but a prostitute. Hogan is angered at having been duped, but he quickly accepts and understands the necessity of the ruse when Sara points out, "If I hadn't been a nun you wouldn't have saved me from those men in the first place."

This aspect of the narrative is well written and well played. The little quirks of the Sara character that are not nunlike (often getting bemused double-take reactions from Hogan) are subtle to make the revelation that she is really a prostitute surprising.

Two Mules for Sister Sara concludes with a battle scene that is effectively shot and edited; Siegel concentrated mostly on medium shots, especially those featuring Eastwood framed by fire on either side and in the background as he engages in battle alongside the Mexicans. The use of Ennio Morricone's music for the first time since the Leone westerns adds greater effect to the action and violence of this scene.[1] As the battle concludes with the Mexicans victorious, Hogan receives a portion of the strongbox as promised. He and Sara ride off together.

The fact that this film concludes with the unlikely partnership maintaining to the end of the movie, and with the indication that it will continue, is rather offbeat. Eastwood's characters nearly always open as loners and remain as such at the end, even when a partnership is formed (and often these partners end up dying before the conclusion of the movie).

There was a great deal of tension on the set of this movie. Clint Eastwood recalled for Richard Schickel that "Shirley was a doll," while MacLaine, in her autobiography, stated, "I loved Clint." But her feelings toward director Don Siegel were another thing. MacLaine is said to be an actress who questions the director's ideas and vision in the most minute detail, which ended up causing increasing tension between her and Siegel. Along with the aforementioned rattlesnake sequence, MacLaine also balked when Siegel wanted her to dismount from her burro on the right side, stating it was improper to do so. However, if she dismounted from the left, she would not be in frame. This resulted in a heated argument on the set with both actress and director walking off and suspending production. They solved their differences in a private meeting.

Two Mules for Sister Sara only returned a very modest box office profit, but the film received favorable reviews. Roger Ebert stated for the *Chicago Sun Times*:

> Don Siegel's *Two Mules for Sister Sara* is a step or two above the usual
> Clint Eastwood Western. To be sure, it has plenty of the obligatory
> Eastwood violence, and the conventional scene of Eastwood lighting

dynamite sticks with his cigar. But that's OK. One of the pleasures of movies is seeing stars doing their thing.

This time, though, there's more to the movie than Eastwood's schtick. Siegel is a first-rate action director (*Coogan's Bluff, Riot in Cell Block 11*), with a knack for directing violence so that it's more exhilarating than disturbing. And his writer, Albert Maltz, has laid a human and funny story on top of the obligatory Eastwood scenes so *Two Mules* is successful on a couple of levels . . . the movie is a lot better than it might have been. Miss Shirley MacLaine sparkles in an essentially comic role. . . . The Maltz dialog is funny and has a nice cynical edge to it, and the fort is blown up with a suitable flourish. And somewhere along the way, Eastwood demonstrates that silent comedy isn't entirely dead.

Roger Greenspun in the *New York Times* stated:

Directed by Don Siegel after a story by Budd Boetticher, *Two Mules for Sister Sara*, which opened yesterday at the Cinerama Theater, ought to be the realization of a movie lover's dream. And, by the happiest juxtapositions of imagination and talent, it is. I'm not sure that it is a great movie, but it is very good, and it stays and grows in the mind the way only movies of exceptional narrative intelligence do. Intelligence is the operative word; for although the film is also charming, funny, cruel, sad and occasionally quite terrifying, it is by the richness and complex vigor with which it combines events, ideas, images and people that it chiefly lives.

In its development of major themes and minor preoccupations *Two Mules for Sister Sara* sounds mostly like the work of Don Siegel (*Coogan's Bluff, Madigan, Hell Is for Heroes*, etc.), and in its narrative shapeliness it feels very much like Budd Boetticher (a fine and somewhat neglected filmmaker). I have no idea that the two men collaborated, but I am very glad that both names are involved.

Bridget Byrne said in a review by the *Los Angeles Herald-Examiner, Two Mules for Sister Sara* was called

a solidly entertaining film that provides Clint Eastwood with his best, most substantial role to date; in it he is far better than he has ever been. In director Don Siegel, Eastwood has found what John Wayne found in John Ford and what Gary Cooper found in Frank Capra.

Clint Eastwood won the Laurel Award for Best Action performance. Shirley MacLaine was nominated but did not win.

Two Mules for Sister Sara remains a good western film in the evolution of Clint Eastwood's work in the genre. There are many elements it contains that would later inform his self-directed movies in this genre.

Upon completing *Two Mules for Sister Sara*, Eastwood was put in the military comedy *Kelly's Heroes*, which was yet another big production in which the actor saw initial potential that eventually dissipated by its conclusion. However, his following film, *The Beguiled* (1971), was yet another reinvention of the western movie theme—a Civil War story that was to be the most complex film he'd appeared in up to that time.

Note

1. Morricone's score for this film actually became one of his most well-known works. A couple pieces of music from this film were also used in Quentin Tarantino's *Django Unchained* (2012).

CHAPTER 9

The Beguiled (1971)

(Produced by the Malpaso Company for Universal Studios)
Director: Don Siegel
Screenplay: Albert Maltz (billed as John B. Sherry) and Irene Kamp (billed as Grimes Grice); from the novel by Thomas Cullinan
Producer: Don Siegel
Associate Producer: Claude Traverse
Executive Producers: Clint Eastwood, Jennings Lang
Music: Lalo Schifrin
Cinematography: Bruce Surtees
Editing: Carl Pingitore
Cast: Clint Eastwood (John McBurney), Geraldine Page (Martha), Elizabeth Hartman (Edwina), Jo Ann Harris (Carol), Darleen Carr (Doris), Mae Mercer (Hallie), Pamelyn Ferdin (Amy), Melody Thomas (Abigail), Peggy Drier (Lizzie), Patricia Mattick (Janie), George Dunn (Sam Jefferson), Matt Clark (Scroggins), Patrick Culliton (Miles Farnsworth), Jim Malinda (Wade), Charlie Briggs (1st Confederate Captain), Charles Martin (2nd Confederate Captain), Randy Brown (Confederate Sergeant), Buddy Van Horn (Soldier), Victor Izay (Wagon Driver), Bill Lee (Singer).
Gross: $1,100,000
Release Date: March 31, 1971
Running Time: 105 minutes
Sound Mix: Mono (Westrex Recording System)
Color: Technicolor
Aspect Ratio: 1.85: 1
Availability: DVD (Universal)

The Beguiled is perhaps the most controversial film in this study as it is the one that may be most difficult to justify as a western—even more so than *Coogan's Bluff* (1968) in that the central character in that movie was a lawman from Arizona. *The Beguiled* is a melodrama set in the Civil War South. However, this Don Siegel–Clint Eastwood film is a more artistic look at its setting and the human conflicts that occur therein, and Eastwood's Civil War soldier is another variation of his western character. Also, the studio, Universal, tried to market the film as a western, and some believe that is part of the reason for its disappointing box office returns.

While looking for possible film prospects, Clint Eastwood found himself engrossed by a Thomas Cullinan novel set during the Civil War that producer Jennings Lang had sent to him. He was so intrigued with the story and its characters that he read the novel in one night. Don Siegel had the same reaction when Eastwood handed him the novel to read while they were shooting *Two Mules for Sister Sara* (1970). Eastwood realized that playing the lead role would be far different than anything Eastwood had done before, which could be a potentially dangerous move for an actor whose screen persona was established with his audience. Eastwood was willing to take that chance, believing it could extend his range as an actor. In Richard Schickel's biography he was quoted as saying, "I wasn't sure an audience was ready for that, or wanted that, but I knew I wanted it." Drawn to the complexity of the character, and the narrative, Eastwood called the film "something I could act, something besides just gunning people down."

Don Siegel looked upon the project as a director, realizing what he could do with atmosphere and nuance. It was a seamy story set during the Civil War and has as much to do with the horror/suspense genre as it does with the western genre. Universal Studios marketed this film as a standard Eastwood western, and its Civil War setting may recall *The Good, the Bad, and the Ugly* (1966), but it is certainly offbeat and by no means conventional. It is a nontraditional western story where a Civil War soldier is held prisoner, but not specifically by the enemy.

Eastwood plays John McBurney, an injured Yankee who is found in the woods by a twelve-year-old girl (Pamelyn Ferdin) in Southern territory near an all-girl boarding school. Broken and dying, the enemy soldier is brought by the girls into their boardinghouse with the intention of turning him over to the Confederate army once he has healed. As he gradually recovers due to their care, he utilizes his charms to entice each of their repressed sexual desires, from the headmistress (Geraldine Page) down to the teenaged students. Jealousies arise, while the soldier plots to somehow escape enemy territory once he is able to get away.

Lobby card for *The Beguiled.*

Edward Gallafent stated in *Clint Eastwood: Filmmaker and Star*:

> The mansion and its inhabitants embody a set of familiar elements
> which describe the social order defeated by the Union in the Civil
> War. They are commonly presented in a way which both offers a
> criticism of that order and mourns its passing, and this is true here.
> The building and its furniture, fittings, and artworks present a vision
> of an aristocratic culture implicitly associated with Europeanness and
> a non-Anglophone world—a world seen as both splendid and useless.

The headmistress is angered by his rejecting her and showing more interest
in the schoolteacher (Elizabeth Hartman), so when the soldier takes a fall down
the stairs and is knocked unconscious, the headmistress insists his leg must be
amputated to avoid gangrene. When he awakens and finds his leg is gone, he
goes into a drunken rage, even grabbing the youngest girl's pet turtle and throwing it to the ground, killing it. Remorseful once he sobers up, he apologizes, but

the youngest girl is unforgiving. She feeds him poison mushrooms and he dies. The girls bury him while the teacher stands by weeping as the film concludes.

The Beguiled's opening credits feature sepia images of war and battle, fading into a sepia shot of the little girl picking mushrooms. The picture changes to color by the time she discovers the soldier. Thus, we understand the setting and the situation once the film begins.

The story allowed for a lot of psychological depth for each character, with the soldier as the center of attention. Albert Maltz was hired to write the screenplay, both Siegel and Eastwood having been pleased with his work on *Two Mules for Sister Sara*, but his script rewrote the ending to be upbeat and happy. Eastwood wanted to keep the original story's darker ending where the soldier is poisoned and dies. He liked the idea of the central character's death having no immediate meaning to anyone except the weeping schoolteacher, as if he had never been found and ended up perishing alone in the woods. Siegel agreed, quoted as saying in Schickel's biography of Eastwood, "The whole point of the story—its central irony—was that these females must ultimately prove themselves to be deadlier than the male. Pull off the mask of the innocent virginal nymphs and you will reveal the dark hidden secrets of wily manipulators." The bosses at Universal Studios also balked at the ending, but Siegel and Eastwood insisted on maintaining the integrity of the original novel's darkness. Screenwriter Irene Kamp was asked to rewrite the Maltz script, but her rewrite did not please Siegel or Eastwood. Producer Jennings Lang had associate producer Claude Traverse write a new script that was more faithful to the book. Maltz, and co-writer Irene Kamp, were represented by pseudonyms in the credits. Traverse received no credit for writing at all.

The Beguiled remains a very tense, unsettling film, with the soldier perceived as a sex object due mostly to the repressed desires of the women and the girls. The headmistress has an incestuous past that is revealed at the end, the teacher is sweet and virginal, and the girls are responding to the throes of adolescent angst. The soldier is alternately sexually responsive and manipulatively cagey, but he never appears to be completely in control. Lying in bed, having to have his feet washed by a black housekeeper, the amputation of his leg, and all its Freudian symbolism, keep him imprisoned by his health limitations after his original wounds begin to heal. When Confederate soldiers run by to check on how things are going, they are not told about the Union soldier lying helpless and wounded in the boarding school. The women feel it is their duty to heal his wounds, and then turn him over to their allies. This is not the Clint Eastwood movie character that gets out of situations handily. This character never leaves. He is destroyed by the same child who rescued him.

Siegel shot the film on a plantation in Baton Rouge, Louisiana, making good use of the beautiful Southern scenery and the authentic Old South building in which the boarding school was housed. Some interiors were shot at Universal Studios. Effectively providing the atmospheric quality that provides much of the tension of the narrative, Siegel would always cite *The Beguiled* as the best film he directed.

Unfortunately, it was a film far ahead of its time. While it opened at number 2 at the box office, mostly due to Clint Eastwood's drawing power; within two weeks, it plummeted to number 50. Actress Pamelyn Ferdin recalled in a 1995 interview with the Seattle media magazine *Feminist Baseball*:

> Unfortunately it didn't do well money wise, at the box office. Clint thought he did a good job in that movie and it was a stretch for him because he played an entirely different character. I think he was very much looking forward to having that movie come out and unfortunately I guess it was not distributed very well or something 'cos I think it could have been a lot bigger than it was.

In an interview with the author, Ms. Ferdin stated:

> Since it wasn't a film where Eastwood came out as a hero, and he even died in the movie, I think most fans couldn't, or wouldn't, accept his fate.

Universal was indeed unable to understand how to properly market the film. In some of the posters, Eastwood is holding a gun, even though he doesn't shoot anyone in the entire film except during a brief flashback sequence regarding the war. Other ads hint at a steamy romance, with ad copy stating: "One man . . . seven women . . . in a strange house!" "His love . . . or his life." Along with marketing, some, such as producer Jennings Lang, felt the movie flopped because Clint Eastwood was emasculated in the film. It was the first film in which his character dies at the end (he would not again die at the end of a movie until *Honkytonk Man* (1982) eleven years later—another box office disappointment).

The Beguiled explores many issues and utilizes interesting cinematic techniques to convey aspects of each character's psychology. When the soldier, under the influence of alcohol, lashes out at the black maid with abject bigotry veiled by sexual desire, her face clenches and her body tightens. She quickly recalls being raped by a white slave owner, letting the soldier know she is ready to fight back. Her flashback is very brief, only seconds long, but it allows us enough to understand her frame of reference in response to the soldier's threat. The virginal curiosity of the teacher is offset by the more lurid sexual background of the headmistress. The girls offer a different level of curiosity, their nubile beauty enticing the soldier's base desires. Director Siegel never allows the viewer to relax. There is always a palpable tension. The viewer is forced to remain uncomfortable.

Cinematographer Bruce Surtees, whom Eastwood would employ for most of his movies, was a master at framing dark imagery, and the precise edits in the brief flashback moments by editor Carl Pingitore resulted in his also being used again by both Eastwood and Siegel.

The flashbacks and the headmistress's dream sequence are used very effectively. Rather than being long and taking the focus away from the main plot, they are brief but informative enough to give the viewer ample background on each character, enhancing the plot.

While *The Beguiled* was a big hit in France, where European sensibilities did not require actors to remain typecast and accepted more daring narrative ideas, in the United States the movie was a box office bomb. Earning barely over a million dollars domestically, it remains the poorest grossing film in Clint Eastwood's career. Part of the problem was that the studio marketed the movie as if it were another action-type movie. Thus, the people who might have appreciated a film like *The Beguiled* did not attend it, while the action fans were disappointed.

Critical opinion was a bit more accepting of the finished film than audiences appeared to be, but none of these critics were terribly impressed. Vincent Canby, in the April 1, 1971, issue of the *New York Times*, noted the film's greater complexity but found it more unusual than inspired, stating:

> Donald Siegel's *The Beguiled* sounds simple enough on paper: Clint Eastwood, as a wounded Yankee soldier, charms and then terrorizes the ladies who nurse him back to health at a very peculiar, more or less forgotten, Louisiana seminary during the closing days of the War Between the States. Nothing, however, is as straightforward as it seems in *The Beguiled*, not even its perversities. Take, for example, the lovely opening sequence in which a little, 12-year-old girl comes upon the body of the soldier in the forest. She is, at first, frozen with fear. Through her mind we hear her wonder whether her father died the same way. Cut to the soldier, and through his eyes we see a curious, shapeless child swim into focus. They talk, exchange names, and just before the child helps him to stand, he draws her down beside him and gives her a long, not really friendly kiss on the mouth. She's confused, but immensely happy. The film thus begins as a quite odd Civil War romance, evolves into a battle of the sexes in which the man is more vanquished than victor, and then turns into the kind of grotesque character comedy that might—mistakenly, I think—be identified as gothic horror. There is certainly horror in *The Beguiled*, but it is played for what amounts to an extended, completely silent laugh. In fact, every major character in the movie, with the exception of Eastwood, is a female suffering to a greater or lesser degree from

the need for a man, including the little girl (Pamelyn Ferdin) who first finds the soldier, the precocious 17-year-old (Jo Ann Harris), who seduces Eastwood with the graces of Belle Watling, and the sweet virginal teacher (Elizabeth Hartman), who comes close to being an unequivocally decent person, the only one in the film. The most deprived (ergo, according to Hollywood Freud, the wildest and most dangerous) woman is the seminary's headmistress (Geraldine Page), whose initial flashback, as she stares at the bloody, maggoty soldier, is to the bed in which she and her brother made frenzied, slow-motion love. My favorite fantasy, however, is Miss Page's wine-induced dream in which she, Eastwood and Miss Hartman make love and then assume the positions of a pietà, more exhausted, I suspect, than sorrowing. This is very fancy, outrageous fantasizing from the man who gave us *Riot in Cell Block 11* and *Baby Face Nelson*, and must strike horror in the hearts of those Siegel fans who've made a cult of his objectivity. *The Beguiled* is not, indeed, successful as baroque melodrama, and, towards the end, there are so many twists and turns of plot and character that everything that's gone before is neutralized. People who consider themselves discriminating moviegoers, but who are uncommitted to Mr. Siegel will be hard put to accept it, other than as a sensational, misogynistic nightmare.

The film's aesthetic success has grown since its 1971 release. Kyle Westphal, when programming a film series in Chicago that included *The Beguiled*, told Ben Sachs of the *Chicago Reader*:

> [T]he movie really gets into the idea of Eastwood as a sex object. And it takes it quite seriously, albeit within an exploitation framework. Every scene in the film is just heaving with desire—Eastwood's [character's] desire for these women and also the women's desire for Eastwood—but none of the characters quite understand exactly what they want. These women are at different ages, they expect different things from men, and they're all attracted to this figure. And the movie lays that desire bare. There's no tiptoeing around it. Eastwood had never made a film like this before. Most people were expecting a shoot-'em-up, and the movie plays on this. It's continually trying to make the audience uncomfortable—on the level of character, on the level of history. . . . You know, you have the black maid in the film whom Eastwood thinks he can seduce by virtue of him being a Yankee, but she proves him wrong. Even though the movie is focused on issues of race and sex to an almost obsessive degree, I don't think you can walk away from it saying it's a progressive film or a reactionary film. It's about subverting our expectations, no matter what they are.

It could also be argued that the characters know exactly what they want; that McBurney wants to escape, and isn't really attracted to females. He merely wants to use them for his own means. Meanwhile, the women want him and want to control him.

Along with being pleased with the quality of the finished product, Eastwood also enjoyed the making of the film. At first he was admittedly intimidated by Broadway actress Geraldine Page being cast as the headmistress (Jeanne Moreau was also considered). Eastwood considered an actress the caliber of Page to be out of his league. He relaxed considerably when, upon meeting her, she told him how much she'd enjoyed his work on *Rawhide*. Eastwood is quoted in Schickel's biography as stating:

> She just set an example for all the young players. When a cast is almost entirely female, it is not unusual for things to get a little competitive in the wardrobe, for the makeup to be different every day. Page was such a ballsy actress. She came in and said "this is who I am, this is how I do it," and these other young gals were sort of drawn into it.

Eastwood compared working with her to working with Lee J. Cobb on *Coogan's Bluff* as both actors were "ready to go, right away, ready to roll, no BS. If there are insecurities, they have them under control; they just step right up to bat." Pamelyn Ferdin recalled for the author:

> Geraldine Page got a lot of respect from everyone on the set, but she was very nice and easy to work with. She was one of the reasons I loved making this movie.

The Beguiled continues to be cited among the most powerful films in either Clint Eastwood's or Don Siegel's career, despite it being their most unsuccessful at the box office. It also continues to merit some level of discussion for controversial ideas, such as the mouth kiss the soldier gives the twelve-year-old upon being rescued (actress Pamelyn Ferdin has stated that this was not in the script nor had it been rehearsed, so the shock on her face is real), and for a misogynistic perspective that permeates the narrative. Schickel argues that the ideas are more misanthropic than misogynistic, while he quotes Eastwood as approaching things more matter-of-factly: "You know, he's totally justifiable. What guy wouldn't try to save his life in a situation like that?"

As Dave Kehr stated on the *Chicago Reader* website, *The Beguiled* is a film that should have played art houses rather than neighborhood theaters, and the consensus that includes latter-day critics like Kehr, Eastwood himself, and supporting players like Pamelyn Ferdin is unanimous that the film was poorly marketed.

Eastwood and Siegel dusted themselves off from this experience and collaborated on a new project, featuring the actor as a no-nonsense police detective who defied authority and went on a veritable crusade against all of the fringe social elements that middle America feared. Dirty Harry Callahan would become one of the true iconic figures of American cinema.

CHAPTER 10

Between the Westerns (1968–1971)

In our discussion of Clint Eastwood's western films, it is important to also acknowledge the non-western movies he made, especially since they often inspire each other.

This is, however, not the case with *Where Eagles Dare* (1969), which has been mentioned earlier. Writer Alistair MacLean (*The Guns of Navarone*) completed the script for *Where Eagles Dare* in six weeks, basing it on his novel. Eastwood starred in support of Richard Burton, the two of them calling the film *Where Doubles Dare* due to all the work their stand-ins and stuntmen had to perform. A fair film, it was a box office success, but it is most notable now for its early use of front projection effect, a visual effect that combines foreground action with background footage already filmed.

Eastwood felt there was potential in *Kelly's Heroes* (1970), about a group of World War II soldiers who go AWOL to rob a bank behind enemy lines. Eastwood recalled that director Brian Hutton had put together a much better movie than what was eventually released after the studio tampered with the completed film. The actor believed the subsequent cuts took away a great deal of depth from the characters. Eastwood was disappointed in *Kelly's Heroes*. He felt the film's initial potential had not been reached, and he even offered to do more work on it himself. The cast in this film is so vast none of them, including Eastwood, are given enough attention to develop a character. *Kelly's Heroes* is entertaining, but not outstanding.

However, being an actor dropped into a big studio production does not allow the level of creative input where his past films might inspire or help to interpret his work.

Play Misty for Me (1971) was Eastwood's first feature-length directorial effort, and it became one of his most successful films from both a critical and box office perspective. He had discussed this project with Malpaso co-founder Irving

Leonard, but Leonard's death in 1969 caused the project to be set aside until Eastwood had the opportunity to produce it. Eastwood told Marc Eliot for his book *American Rebel: The Life of Clint Eastwood*:

> After seventeen years of bouncing my head against the wall, hanging around sets, maybe influencing certain camera set-ups with my own opinions, watching actors go through all kinds of hell without any help, and working with both good directors and bad ones, I'm at the point where I'm ready to make my own pictures. I stored away all the mistakes I made and saved up all the good things I learned, and now I know enough to control my own projects and get what I want out of actors.

In one of the first films to deal with stalking, Clint Eastwood plays a radio DJ who frequently receives calls from a woman (Jessica Walter) requesting the pop standard "Misty." He eventually meets the woman, they have sex, and she thereafter stalks him while exhibiting increasingly greater personality disorders. Things get especially unsettling once the DJ rekindles a relationship with an old girlfriend (Donna Mills).

Eastwood and Donna Mills in *Play Misty for Me*.

Eastwood employed cameraman Bruce Surtees and editor Carl Pingitore, who had worked with him on previous films, while his friend Don Siegel was on the set for most of the filming (and even acts in a cameo role), assisting the fledgling director. Learning from Siegel's efficiency, Eastwood produced *Play Misty for Me* (1971) under its million-dollar budget, and several days ahead of schedule. It ended up grossing over $10 million. Nearly all film critics praised Eastwood's directorial debut.

There is at least a tangential connection between *Play Misty for Me* and his westerns. His late night DJ experience casts him as something of a loner, very much his own man, while his being the object of female obsession has some similarities to *The Beguiled* (1971). And while he seems to initially enjoy the attention, the DJ clearly has no interest in committing beyond this any more than his western antihero would make a long-term commitment to a partner or a group.

At the end of 1971, *Dirty Harry* was released and further defined Clint Eastwood's screen image. If the character he had created in the Dollars trilogy was what established his screen persona, Detective Harry Callahan culminated it. Eastwood was attracted to the character's individualism, and his obsession with a sadistic killer's actions. *Dirty Harry* uses elements of the already established

Eastwood as Dirty Harry.

Eastwood action movie persona most effectively. Triumphantly fighting crime with a large gun and handling the weapon with tight accuracy, Harry is a no-nonsense crime fighter who balks at the idea of due process much more angrily than Walt Coogan had in *Coogan's Bluff* (1968). "Well I'm all broken up about that guy's rights," is his disgruntled response to law enforcement's reprimand of his actions in bringing in a killer.

It is intriguing that research has revealed Frank Sinatra was the first choice for the title role, and it was turned down by several actors (including John Wayne) before it got to Eastwood. It is even more bizarre that war-hero-cum-actor Audie Murphy was to play the psychotic Scorpio, but he was killed in a private plane crash before having the opportunity. Actor Andy Robinson played the character as one of the most wonderfully despicable villains in movie history.

As with *Coogan's Bluff*, director Don Siegel and actor Eastwood place their protagonist in the midst of a world with which he is unfamiliar and suspicious. Callahan shows disdain for "college boys," while the film presents a killer who represents the hippie counterculture by manner and appearance. Audience anger is aroused by having the killer Scorpio commit crimes as heinous as kidnapping a teenage girl, yanking out one of her teeth with pliers to send with a ransom note, and burying her alive. When he is finally shot in the leg, whining that he wants a lawyer, Harry walks over and stands on the man's injured leg. His crimes are so atrocious the audience is manipulated into cheering for Callahan's disregard for the killer's rights. Completely disillusioned by the liberalism of the justice system, Harry ends the film by throwing his badge in the river.

Scorpio was based on an actual serial killer in the late 1960s named the Zodiac Killer, who used to contact local newspapers in California. He was never captured. Callahan is said to have been inspired by Zodiac investigator Dave Toschi, who was also the inspiration for Steve McQueen's *Bullitt* (1968). At one point, the Zodiac killer had threatened to hijack a school bus, a scene that does appear in *Dirty Harry* and is one of the most tightly edited, brilliantly directed scenes in any cop movie of its time.

While most critics understood the concept of the film's structure, many were put off by what they believed supported a level of fascism in law enforcement while misrepresenting the counterculture. Feminists protested outside the Dorothy Chandler Pavilion during the 1972 Academy Awards, by holding up banners that read "Dirty Harry is a Rotten Pig." Eastwood responded in interviews by clarifying that the film's intent was to show how the frustrations of police work could explode into the sort of behavior that Harry Callahan exhibited. Many audience members responded from the opposite perspective, believing it was a glorification of a sadistic cop's actions, pointing out that Scorpio was a long-haired stereotype. Neither of these extremes appears to still be attaching itself to the film in the twenty-first century.

Dirty Harry has certainly grown in critical acceptance over a generation, and the film is now considered one of the greatest American films of all time by such publications as *Empire*, the *New York Times*, *Total Film*, *TV Guide*, and *Vanity Fair*, all of which have stated as much in published lists of top movies. *Dirty Harry* has not only lived on successfully, it also helped inform every role Clint Eastwood played for the remainder of his movie career. This movie was the most effective in taking the loner, antihero persona Eastwood had established in his westerns and transferring it to a non-western film. Despite Eastwood being best known for his westerns, *Dirty Harry* is the most iconic of all his films. In the biographical piece "Eastwood: In His Own Words" for the American Film Institute, Eastwood stated:

> I think people jumped to conclusions about *Dirty Harry* without giving the character much thought, trying to attach right-wing connotations to the film that were never really intended. I thought it was a basic kind of drama—what do you do when you believe so much in law and order and coming to the rescue of people and you just have five hours to solve a case? That kind of impossible effort was fun to portray, but I think it was interpreted as a pro-police point of view, as a kind of rightist heroism, at a time in American history when police officers were looked down on as "pigs," as very oppressive people—I'm sure there are some who are, and a lot who aren't. I've met both kinds.

Eastwood then returned to westerns, but this next one, *Joe Kidd* (1972), offered some differences. Not only was it a much more conventional film, and directed by classic western director John Sturges, it also featured Eastwood playing a character who had as much in common with Harry Callahan as he had with Joe, Manco, or Blondie. Once again an outcast who uses his situation to exact his own agenda, the title character of *Joe Kidd* is defiant of the law (even when acting in its favor) and maintains the detached sarcasm that described nearly all of Eastwood's screen characters at this time. Impressed with Elmore Leonard's screenplay and working with a director like Sturges, Clint Eastwood began filming another western movie.

CHAPTER 11

Joe Kidd (1972)

(Produced by the Malpaso Company for Universal Studios)
Director: John Sturges
Screenplay: Elmore Leonard
Producer: Sidney Beckerman
Executive Producers: Robert Daley, Clint Eastwood, Jennings Lang
Music: Lalo Schifrin
Cinematography: Bruce Surtees
Editing: Ferris Webster
Cast: Clint Eastwood (Joe Kidd), Robert Duvall (Frank Harlan), John Saxon
(Luis Chama), Don Stroud (Lamarr), Stella Garcia (Helen Sanchez),
James Wainwright (Mingo), Paul Koslo (Roy), Gregory Walcott (Mitchell), Dick Van Patten (Hotel Manager), Lynne Marta (Elma), John Carter
(Judge), Pepe Hern (Priest), Joaquin Martinez (Manolo), Rob Soble (Ramon), Pepe Callahan (Naco), Clint Ritchie (Calvin), Gil Barreto (Emilio),
Maria Val (Vita), Chuck Hayward (Eljay), Michael R. Horst (Deputy), Rick
Kahana (Altar Boy), Read Morgan (Cowboy), Ed Deemer (Bartender),
Steve Moriarty (Citizen).
Gross: $6,330,000 (USA)
Release Date: July 14, 1972
Running Time: 88 minutes
Sound Mix: Mono (Westrex Recording System)
Color: Technicolor
Aspect Ratio: 2.35: 1
Availability: DVD and Blu-ray (Universal)

Perhaps what most stands out about *Joe Kidd* is its conventional narrative structure. While the western films Clint Eastwood had done up to this point tended to challenge the genre's standards and basics, *Joe Kidd* is quite ordinary. Eastwood draws from the Harry Callahan character as well as his past western roles.

Poster for *Joe Kidd*.

While considering different projects as his next film, Eastwood was given the script for *Joe Kidd* by producer Jennings Lang. Originally called *The Sinola Courthouse Raid*, Eastwood was impressed that the script was written by novelist Elmore Leonard, whose western novels were often turned into movies, including *Hombre* (1967) and *3:10 to Yuma* (1955, and, later, a 2007 remake). The director chosen was John Sturges, whose past westerns included *Escape from Fort Bravo* (1953), *Gunfight at the O.K. Corral* (1957), *The Law and Jake Wade* (1958), *Last Train from Gun Hill* (1959), and his masterpiece in the genre, *The Magnificent Seven* (1960). With a screenplay by Elmore Leonard, a director like John Sturges, and an actor like Clint Eastwood in the title role, much more is expected than *Joe Kidd* delivers. While not a bad film, it could be considered his least interesting western.

The opening scene features Eastwood as the title character, resting well into the background of a jail cell, with two other prisoners in the foreground. When the guards approach the cell, they address Kidd, asking if he wants breakfast. The other prisoners are disdainful, one being especially vocal, dismissing Kidd as a drunk.

> Joe Kidd: Bob Mitchell hit me?
>
> Guard: Yes.
>
> Joe Kidd: Anyone else?
>
> Guard: No.

Kidd finds that he is handcuffed to the bed. He is not released until it is his turn to go before the judge. As he gets up, the more vocal prisoner hands him a pan of stew and says, "Guero, you want some?" Kidd casually takes the pan and dumps the stew over the prisoner's head. He gets up, and Kidd smacks him with the pan.

Eastwood establishes his character very quickly. He is not intimidated by his surroundings or the people who inhabit his immediate world, as in his usual western movie persona. He also exhibits a compulsive violence that is sudden and jarring, as Harry Callahan might have displayed. With little effort and an economy of movement, Joe Kidd controls his environment.

Kidd is taken before the judge by Bob Mitchell (Gregory Walcott), the lawman who hit him, prompting this dialogue as they go:

> Joe Kidd: You shouldn't have hit me, Bob.
>
> Mitchell: Next time I'll knock your damn head off.

Kidd retains this sarcastic demeanor once he is before the judge's bench.

Judge: It's against the law to hunt on reservation land.

Kidd: The deer didn't know where he was, and I wasn't sure either.

Given the option of a ten-dollar fine or ten days in jail, the penniless Kidd takes the ten days.

Through most of the film, Joe Kidd is caught between two factions. First, he listens patiently as Luis Chama (John Saxon) and his people storm the courtroom, hold the judge at gunpoint, and make a statement about how white landowners have taken over land that rightfully belongs to the Mexican people, but a fire destroyed any evidence proving that. In a bold move, Kidd takes the judge out of the courtroom as the argument goes nowhere, and helps him escape danger. Chama and the peasants he has gathered decide to wage a war against the landowners.

Sturges films this nicely, mostly in medium shots, cutting away from Chama to the judge. He uses close-ups of a quietly intrigued Joe Kidd on the sidelines more sparingly. Joe Kidd is attentive but still removed.

Wealthy landowner Frank Harlan (Robert Duvall) forms a posse to capture Chama, springing Joe Kidd from prison and asking him to join. Joe refuses, having no personal issues with the bandit. However, when Joe discovers Chama's men have raided his own ranch, he changes his mind and joins Harlan's posse. When Harlan takes the Mexican villagers hostage and threatens to kill them unless Chama surrenders, Kidd realizes he may be on the wrong side. He saves the hostages and separates from Harlan, deciding to bring Chama in himself, realizing that his own issues with the bandit must result in his being brought to justice. When Kidd does capture Chama and brings him in, he discovers Harlan is already in town waiting. Kidd drives a locomotive into the town saloon as a distraction, then engages in a gunfight with Harlan's men, killing them all. Harlan is eventually killed in the courthouse by Kidd, who is hiding in the judge's chair.

The conflict between land grabbers and the Mexican people is a classic western movie conflict. Both writer Leonard and director Sturges were certainly up to the task of creating a strong film from this idea. The plot, with its two rival factions, vaguely resembles *A Fistful of Dollars* (1964), except here Joe Kidd takes a more definite side in the battle rather than playing the two against each other. Sturges was a no-nonsense director who had his ideas set and ready when he showed up for filming each day and, as a result, got along famously with Clint Eastwood, as this was the actor's preferred method of working. Leonard's script was often rewritten by the producer, but the screenwriter would then cross out the producer's corrections and put back his own ideas before presenting it to Eastwood and director Sturges.

Unfortunately, as stated earlier in the text, *Joe Kidd* can only be described as disappointing when one considers the talent involved. It is a moderately effective pedestrian western. According to Richard Schickel's biography,

> [Sturges] had always wanted to do a train wreck. . . . The idea kept gnawing at him, and one day he proposed that they fire up the engine and, with Clint at the controls, run it right off the track, through some outbuildings and into the bar where the subsidiary bad guys were gathered. It would, he said, make a very photogenic mess. So it was done, and in its way it worked. It made no sense, but it put an exclamation point of sorts on the picture.

Eastwood was having some health issues during the shooting of this movie, including a bronchial infection. The press reported it was due to an allergy to horses, which might have been amusing irony, but it wasn't true. While filming *Joe Kidd*, the success of *Dirty Harry* (1971) started to emerge; Eastwood stated in interviews that it was at this point in time when he finally started to feel truly secure in his acting career.

Joe Kidd was an aesthetic comedown from *Dirty Harry* by not living up to its promising potential. Roger Greenspun in the *New York Times* stated:

> For perhaps its first half-hour, John Sturges's new Western, *Joe Kidd*, looks surprisingly good. It seems restrained, relaxed, unfashionably out of the current mode in its commitment to people and horses rather than to sadistic monsters and machines. Nothing remarkable, but modestly decent—a feeling that persists, with continually diminishing assurance, almost until the climax, when everything is thrown away in a flash of false theatrics, foolish symbolism and what I suspect is sloppy editing.
>
> That "everything" is indeed a fairly conventional story about land rights in New Mexico at the turn of the century. There is an evil land baron (Robert Duvall), a leader of the people (John Saxon), a beautiful woman of high principle (Stella Garcia), and an enigmatic loner (Clint Eastwood) who really determines the action. In a very mild way, the film supports the rights of a dispossessed Mexican minority. But no matter what the particular sympathies, politics in westerns tends toward autocracy, and *Joe Kidd* ends with Clint Eastwood as judge, jury, and executioner in a killing that is of course supposed to change the moral nature of the world.
>
> Like so many western heroes, Joe Kidd figures even in his own time as an anachronism—powerful through his instincts mainly, and through the ability of everybody else, whether in rage or gratitude, to recognize in him a quality that must be called virtue. The great value of Clint Eastwood in such a position is that he guards his virtue very

cannily, and in the society of "Joe Kidd," where the men still manage to tip their hats to the ladies (but just barely), all the Eastwood effects and mannerisms suggest a carefully preserved authenticity.

It is a very good performance in context. Ultimately, it is the only real point of interest to *Joe Kidd*, and especially interesting because in recent years the Eastwood point of view has appeared mostly as ancillary to the larger vision of director Don Siegel (*Dirty Harry*, *The Beguiled* [1971], among others). What emerges here is a kind of authoritative normalcy, an actor's gift to an ordinary film that at least gives him reasonable space to breathe.

Roger Ebert of the *Chicago Sun Times* wrote:

All I can tell you about Clint Eastwood in *Joe Kidd* is that he plays a ruthless gunman of few words. This isn't exactly a surprise; Eastwood almost always plays a ruthless gunman, etc. The funny thing about *Joe Kidd*, though, is that we can't keep straight whose side he's on, or why. Let's see. The movie opens with Eastwood in jail. He's sprung by a wealthy landowner who needs a hired killer. The landowner wants to go after Luis Chama (John Saxon), charismatic revolutionary leader of the Mexicans (who claim the land is really theirs). Eastwood won't go. But then Chama ties one of Eastwood's men to a fence with barbed wire. I think Eastwood said it was one of his men. But men of what? Does Eastwood own a ranch? Run an army? His occupation is never made clear. Must be something you need men for, anyway. Why Chama tied the guy with the barbed wire is also not made very clear, but I have a theory. It was to keep Eastwood in the movie. See, Eastwood had already refused to join the posse and had gone back to jail. So unless Chama did something, the movie would have continued without Eastwood, and there is not a big market these days for John Saxon Westerns, especially when Saxon doesn't even play a cowboy. Anyway, they go out on the manhunt. But then the landowner turns out to be so evil that barbed wire is a positive blessing compared to him. He decides to shoot five villagers every six hours until Chama surrenders. Meanwhile, he fires Eastwood (I'm not sure why) and locks him in the church with the villagers. Then there are some neat scenes where Eastwood bushwhacks a couple of the landowner's boys. And there are plenty of gunfights all the way through, of course. The director is John Sturges, who has made infinitely better films than this one (*The Great Escape*, *Bad Day at Black Rock*). He seems to have bogged down. The photography is undeniably beautiful, but there comes a point when we've had too many mountains and too little plot. All that holds the movie together is the screen persona of Eastwood, who is so convincingly tight-lipped that sometimes you have the feeling he knows what's

going on and just won't tell. One of the puzzling aspects of *Joe Kidd*
is the buried political content. The Mexican revolutionary leader
seems to have been modeled on Castro and Che, and he has a couple
of speeches like: "It doesn't matter if the people die; they will die
anyway unless our revolution succeeds." Then, at the end, he actually
allows himself to be talked into turning himself in and counting on
a fair trial! Maybe this is the first revolutionary Western made for a
special screening at the White House.

Joe Kidd is actually rather entertaining as one is watching it, but if one tends to
overthink the plot, as Ebert proves here, it really doesn't make much sense.

Perhaps because it worked in other settings, there is a tangential romantic
subplot with Chama's woman Helen (Stella Garcia) with whom he leaves town
at the end of the movie. Once again there is little development here, and it
seems like it was plopped in for Joe Kidd to have a romantic interest. It is not so
completely distanced and distracted as the romance in *Hang 'Em High* (1968),
as it has a more organic connection to the narrative in regard to the central protagonist, but it never feels completely necessary.

Joe Kidd's original source material may have been the story of Reies López
Tijerina, who led a raid on the Tierra Amarilla courthouse on June 5, 1967. Elmore Leonard could have been inspired by this actual occurrence, as it was one
of the most dramatic events of its time. Tijerina was concerned about the rights
of the Hispanic people, and he was instrumental in organizing them in attempts
to obtain their original land grant claims. In the movie *Joe Kidd*, Luis Chama
(John Saxon) organizes a similar revolt against Anglo landowners.

Joe Kidd is not so much a bad movie as it is a disappointing one when considering the level of talent involved. And, in comparison to Eastwood's other
westerns, it is both the most conventional as well as being one of the least interesting. This is not to say that Eastwood couldn't function in a more standard
western setting. *Pale Rider* (1985) probably comes closest to that.

With the success of *Play Misty for Me* (1971), Clint Eastwood set his sights
on doing more directing. His next western, *High Plains Drifter* (1973), was the
first he would direct in the genre. It would exhibit all he had learned from such
mentors as Sergio Leone, Don Siegel, Ted Post, and John Sturges. It would also
more clearly present his cinematic vision regarding the western film.

CHAPTER 12

High Plains Drifter (1973)

(A Malpaso Production for Universal Studios)
Director: Clint Eastwood
Screenplay: Ernest Tidyman, Dean Riesner
Producer: Robert Daley
Executive Producer: Jennings Lang
Music: Dee Barton
Cinematography: Bruce Surtees
Editing: Ferris Webster
Cast: Clint Eastwood (The Stranger), Verna Bloom (Sarah Belding), Billy Curtis (Mordecai), Marianna Hill (Callie Travers), Mitchell Ryan (Dave Drake), Jack Ging (Morgan Allen), Stefan Gierasch (Mayor Jason Hobart), Ted Hartley (Lewis Belding), Geoffrey Lewis (Stacey Bridges), Scott Walker (Bill Borders), Walter Barnes (Sheriff Sam Shaw), Paul Brinegar (Lutie Naylor), Richard Bull (Asa Goodwin), Robert Donner (Preacher), John Hillerman (Bootmaker), Jack Kosslyn (Saddlemaker), Anthony James (Cole Carlin), John Quade (Jake Ross), Dan Vadis (Dan Carlin), James Gosa (Tommy Morris), Russ McCubbin (Fred Short), Belle Mitchell (Mrs. Lake), Buddy Van Horn (Marshal Jim Duncan), John Mitchum (Warden), William O'Connell (Barber), Jane Aull (Townswoman), Carl C. Pitti (Teamster), Chuck Waters (Stableman), Jimmie Booth (Target Wagon Driver), Alex Tinne (Bit).
Budget: $5.5 million
Gross: $15,700,000
Release date: August 22, 1973
Running Time: 105 minutes
Sound Mix: Mono (Westrex Recording System)
Color: Technicolor
Aspect Ratio: 2.35: 1
Availability: DVD and Blu-ray (Universal)

High Plains Drifter is Clint Eastwood's second feature film as a director, and it is his first self-directed western. Immediately upon the opening scene, we can spot how his strongest directorial influences—Sergio Leone and Don Siegel—inspired his own directorial style. Wisely choosing the keen eye of veteran art director Henry Bumstead, who presents a desolate area where a makeshift town is operating, Eastwood films himself from several angles, the central character trotting in on horseback, the town's backdrop providing an eerie negative space. Eastwood's edits are quick, but still revealing. The reactions of the onlookers who stare at him indicate that a stranger riding through is both unusual and unwelcome. Onlookers are shown with a moving camera panning along several people, the edits alternating between medium shots, close-ups, and a nice overhead angle that shows the stranger on his horse—the lone moving figure framed by the town and its people. There are shots from the stranger's vantage point. There are close-ups of single figures as well as groups, introducing us to

Poster for *High Plains Drifter*.

those who will be a part of the narrative. The soundtrack offers only the blowing winds. This quiet, carefully paced opening is jarringly interrupted by the sound of a whip crack and the noise of a horse and wagon riding off. That sound fades into the wind as the stranger patiently ties his horse to a hitching post.

The strength of this opening sequence nicely displays Eastwood's creative artistry as a director. This ride through town offers so many different angles, that Eastwood had to arrange several setups to film the scene according to his vision. There is no distraction, nothing disconcerting about his method. With cinematographer Surtees and editor Webster, Eastwood provides a nice, evenly flowing opening that offers the precise tension necessary for the effectiveness of the narrative. The lack of music and dialogue in this opening also sets up the eerie tone that persists throughout the entire film.

This tension extends to the saloon the stranger enters upon hitching up his horse. Three men indicate his presence is unwelcome. They make a threat; he brushes it off—with the same level of dismissive sarcasm that was by now a fixture of his screen persona—has his drink, and leaves. The stranger settles into a barber shop for a shave and a bath. The three men enter and surround him as he sits lathered in a barber chair. In another characteristic reaction, he reveals a gun tucked under the barber's apron and easily blows the men away. The narrative is described as the stranger is bathing. The sheriff comes in and explains that those he shot were hired killers to protect the town from the Carlin brothers, who have just been released from prison. These men swore revenge on the town for their being sentenced. The sheriff indicates the stranger will not be arrested for the murders if he agrees to take their place and protect the town. In order to entice the stranger, the sheriff indicates he can have anything he wants without having to pay.

There are several elements to consider as the narrative is established. First, the power given to the stranger has some similarities to Eastwood's supervision of this production as its director. The stranger reinvents the town according to his personal vision; he has everything painted red, changes the town's name from Lago to Hell, has a man's barn dismantled to make picnic benches, and has the entire hotel evacuated so he can operate from there. This causes friction from Belding (Ted Hartley), the owner of the barn and hotel, but the stranger maintains his stoic composure, despite much of the town wondering about why he wants to put together a massive barbecue to welcome the Carlin brothers to town. As a final act, the stranger makes a town midget he has befriended, Mordecai (Billy Curtis), the new sheriff and mayor.

The stranger is the director and the townspeople are the actors who must comply; despite their questioning his perspective, they do as he says and he does not need to explain himself. There are parallels here, whether or not they were intended.

The way the specifics of the Carlin brothers and their conflict with the town are presented is one of the more artistically intriguing aspects of the film. While the stranger sleeps, he dreams about the Carlin brothers mercilessly whipping Marshal Duncan (Buddy Van Horn, the film's stunt coordinator) as the town stands by and allows it to happen. It is indicated that Duncan's being whipped to death had been arranged by corrupt town leaders, but thereafter the town allowed the Carlins to be arrested for it. They are now returning for vengeance. As the narrative progresses, we come to realize the dream is, in fact, what happened.

Some of the stranger's leadership is played for comedy. He comes into a saloon and orders drinks for the house. When presented with a bill, he informs that he doesn't have to pay. The townsfolk are pleased with the free whiskey, but the bartender is not. During a sequence where the stranger attempts to train the townspeople to defend themselves, he has a wagon filled with dummies led through town by a team of horses. The people shoot at the dummies and continue to miss each time. Finally, the frustrated stranger pulls out his gun and easily blows the dummies away.

Eastwood's direction does an effective job of balancing this humorous scene within the context of a dramatic narrative by presenting that while he attempts to train the population's marksmanship, the Carlin brothers are shooting three men, stealing their horses, and heading to town. Also, the town leaders who had originally wanted the stranger as protection are now having second thoughts because he is completely taking over according to his own ideas and not kowtowing to their interests. They arrange to have the stranger ambushed at the hotel, but he outwits them and kills all but one. The hotel is destroyed during the disruption.

The stranger is mysterious, he is controlling, he is all-knowing, and he is powerful. When he converses with Belding's wife (Verna Bloom), she indicates that the marshal was buried in an unmarked grave, stating, "the dead don't rest without a marker."

Believing he has everything set up, and unable to trust the people who hired him, the stranger rides out of town, leaving behind the townsfolk stationed on roofs with rifles. The Carlin brothers ride in and have no trouble with the poor marksmanship of these people; the brothers effectively take over the town with few shots fired, which kill the corrupt leaders whom they have most specifically targeted. They burn down the town, keeping the few surviving townspeople in the saloon. The stranger returns and is confronted by Dan Carlin (Dan Vadis) whom he overpowers and whips to death with Carlin's own whip. Upon doing so, he tosses the whip into the saloon. As it falls to the floor, it alerts the two surviving brothers, each of whom confront the stranger, and each of whom is killed by him.

In one of the most creative choices Eastwood makes as a director, the stranger is shown riding through town the next day in the same stark manner in which he had ridden in. Again there are several angles, but the background is even more desolate, as the town has now been reduced to debris. Belding emerges from the shadows in an attempt to shoot the stranger but is shot to death by an observant Mordecai instead. When the stranger does depart, he rides near the graveyard where Mordecai is carving a grave marker. The midget addresses him:

> Mordecai: I never knew your name.
>
> Stranger: Yes, you do.

The camera reveals the graver marker is for Marshal Jim Duncan. The stranger rides off and his image fades as if vanishing into the atmosphere.

When Clint Eastwood first read the story treatment for *High Plains Drifter*, he was intrigued by the supernatural element and the offbeat approach, realizing it was influenced by the sort of European western that he'd helped establish. Arranging a joint production between his company Malpaso and Universal Studios, Eastwood hired Oscar-winning screenwriter Ernest Tidyman, who had been awarded for penning the script for *The French Connection* (1971). Dean Riesner again made an uncredited contribution. Tidyman fleshed out the idea with the sort of black humor Leone liked to use, and he understood the underlying allegorical perspective of the original story as well.

Eastwood chose to shoot *High Plains Drifter* near Mono Lake, which was hundreds of miles from Hollywood in Mono, California. Eastwood employed approximately forty technicians and several construction workers who built the set—consisting of fourteen houses and one two-story hotel—in under twenty days. Eastwood wanted to shoot interiors on location, so complete buildings, not facades, were constructed. The movie was filmed in narrative sequence and was completed ahead of schedule and under budget. It became the sixth highest grossing western of the 1970s.

Eastwood told Peter Byskind in a 1993 article in *Premiere* that *High Plains Drifter* incurred a negative reaction from John Wayne when Eastwood sent the veteran actor a request to do a movie together. Wayne expressed his disdain in a return letter to Eastwood that stated, "[*High Plains Drifter*] isn't what the West was all about. That isn't the American people who settled this country." Eastwood explained to Howard Hughes in his book *Aim for the Heart*: "[I]t's just an allegory . . . a speculation on what happens when they go ahead and kill the sheriff and somebody comes back and calls the town's conscience to bear. There's always retribution for your deeds."

It can be argued that *High Plains Drifter* is the more realistic version of what the west was really like, as opposed to the romanticized John Wayne westerns. The American west was a violent place that was difficult to live in, where people lived far enough away from the nation's government to feel comfortable abiding by their own rules and their own definitions of justice; that is the kind of world this film depicts.

According to Patrick McGilligan, Arthur Knight in *Saturday Review* remarked that Eastwood had "absorbed the approaches of Siegel and Leone and fused them with his own paranoid vision of society," and while this was essentially considered a negative reaction, it is accurate, and positive. The inspiration that Eastwood drew from these directors, as well as from Ted Post or John Sturges, did inform his own methods, and he responded effectively to the allegorical perspective of the screenplay.

There are some unsettling areas. When the town prostitute (Marianna Hill) purposely bumps into the stranger in an attempt to meet him, he grabs her by the wrist, drags her into a barn, and rapes her. Her angry reaction is for naught, as he has been given carte blanche to indulge in whatever he wants without concern for repercussion. He forms a similar connection to Belding's wife, although this is consensual despite initial protests.

It can be argued that the stranger has an initial contempt for the people of this town, and his presence (or his return, depending on one's perspective) is for vengeance. When the prostitute violently bumps into him, he responds with violence. Part of this scene's purpose is apparently to show how far the stranger's power reaches, and how he is the complete opposite of the traditional western hero, but the scene remains unnecessary and off-putting. The stranger's traits are apparent without this scene, which just makes him a little less compelling to watch. Eastwood has stated in several later interviews that if he made the film nowadays, he would not have used that scene.

High Plains Drifter takes issue with the hypocrisy of the western hero stereotype in a manner that is even more explicit than any of the Leone films. The hero is supplanted by the antihero. The stranger expresses little as he rides into the small mining town. It is a full six minutes before he speaks, despite being in the movie from its very outset. The people are suspicious, guilty, ashamed, and openly hostile. There are no good guys here. The good guy was brutally murdered as the town watched. This is what rises from that incident. The townspeople are as much the villains of the film as the Carlin brothers. The impending threat of the Carlins is the instigator that allows the stranger to take over the town and teach the townsfolk a lesson—it is they against whom he wars.

The dynamic that connects is the very tall stranger and the diminutive Mordecai, whom he perceives as an outsider. He is made into a leader as the gunslinging stranger is given supervision of the town. Billy Curtis recalled for the author in an interview:

Clint Eastwood gave me the best role of my career. The only problem is, I got a stiff neck from having to keep looking up at him! No kidding! But it was worth it to be in one of the best western pictures ever made.

Eastwood had some fun with his direction, including using his stuntman Buddy Van Horn as the ghostly stranger's lifetime counterpart. During the final scene in the cemetery, among the grave markers include S. Leone and D. Siegel. Even on the set, after the town was renamed Hell, Eastwood would frequently instruct the cast and crew to "go to hell" when shooting would resume after a break. Verna Bloom recalled his kindness, stating in Richard Schickel's biography of Eastwood that part of the filming conflicted with her wedding plans, and Eastwood agreed to shoot around her with a double. She also stated that despite directing himself, he was never disengaged as an actor: "When he was doing a scene he was just as much involved as anyone else."

There has been some discussion as to the identity of the stranger. The script originally indicated that the stranger was the marshal's brother, and scenes alluding to this were filmed, but Eastwood had them excised. In the released film, the stranger is more of a ghostly figure, perhaps a reincarnation of Duncan, based

Eastwood and Billy Curtis.

on the final lines between him and Mordecai and the supernatural air about the story.

Most of the film deals with a warped perspective on social realities, and Eastwood's approach to this mind-set has clearly been an inspiration to later filmmakers like Tim Burton and Quentin Tarantino, each of whom also use dark humor within a dramatic context that deals in behavioral extremes and a revisionist approach to conventional ideas.

The *New York Times* stated:

> *High Plains Drifter*, with Eastwood as director as well as star, is part ghost story, part revenge Western, more than a little silly, and often quite entertaining in a way that may make you wonder if you have lost your good sense. The violence of the film (including a couple of murders by bull-whipping) is continual and explicit. It exalts and delights in a kind of pitiless Old Testament wrath. However, it is also apparent that neither Ernest Tidyman, who wrote the screenplay, nor Eastwood are taking themselves too seriously. Eastwood's character-ization of The Stranger, who settles God's score with Lago, is a high parody of the soft-featured, brutal Man With No Name he played in those bitter Sergio Leone Westerns. Tidyman's dialogue is funny, and the physical setting—some weather beaten shacks on the edge of a body of water that looks like a dead sea—is startlingly beautiful.

Regarding this review's contention that there are similarities to the characters Eastwood played in the Leone westerns, the stranger does indeed play a Man with No Name, and his manner of dress is quite like Joe, Manco, or Blondie. However, the stranger in this film seems to be working for a higher purpose than his own.

The fact that Clint Eastwood followed the conventional western *Joe Kidd* with the unconventional *High Plains Drifter* indicates his interest in examining different approaches to long-standing cinematic traditions. The financial success his films were now enjoying allowed Eastwood to investigate other ideas, and while he remained active, he would not do another western for three more years. This was a period of exploration for Eastwood as both an actor and a filmmaker. The western genre that had become the foundation of his screen work, as well as the elevated status he had received from the enormous success of *Dirty Harry* (1971), continued to inform every subsequent project.

CHAPTER 13

Between the Westerns (1973–1976)

By 1973, Clint Eastwood established himself as a top box office star, primarily due to the strength of *Dirty Harry* (1971) and the rerelease of his Leone westerns (sometimes in double and triple features at the drive-in). Many critics recognized the effectiveness of his economy of movement and the artistic potential of his directorial vision. Others were unable to appreciate what he was offering, disturbed, perhaps, by the lack of convention in his work and his choice to play a character that was low key. According to Howard Hughes, the *San Francisco Chronicle* called Eastwood "one of the most limited actors on screen." For its review of *Hang 'Em High* (1968), the *Daily Express* quipped, "Eastwood made his first talkie." Critic Rex Reed dismissed *Play Misty for Me* (1971) as "*Psycho* in mothballs" and called *High Plains Drifter* (1973) "one of the year's most hysterical comedies." The fact remains that these films have all held up, as has Eastwood's career, and as late as the twenty-first century, the octogenarian is considered one of the finest American filmmakers of his era. Clint Eastwood fits into the oft-used cliché of being "ahead of his time."

In 1973 Eastwood chose to direct a film in which he did not star. The result was the romantic drama *Breezy* focusing on the May–December romance between characters played by eighteen-year-old Kay Lenz and fifty-something William Holden. Breezy (Lenz) is an inquisitive, guitar-wielding hippie stereotype who is capable of unconditional love without attachment, while Frank (Holden) is a jaded, cynical recluse of the business world. She calls him "black cloud," and eventually he responds to her youthful vitality. It is an interesting counterpart to *Play Misty for Me*, and the actors, including a strong supporting cast that includes Roger C. Carmel and Marj Dusay, are excellent. An overlooked film in the Eastwood canon, *Breezy* effectively brings us to the era of free love and the generation gap in a tasteful, insightful drama helped by Eastwood's choice of shots and how he presents each character.

Eastwood followed this with *Magnum Force* (1973), the sequel to *Dirty Harry*. And while it made more money than its predecessor, it remains, aesthetically, the weakest of the Harry Callahan films. Director Ted Post recalled for the author:

> I was looking forward to working with Clint again. Our careers went in different directions since we did *Hang 'Em High*, but both were rising. He'd become a big star, and mostly because of *Dirty Harry*, so I figured if I directed the sequel, my career would soar into the big time. It turned out to be maybe the worst experience of my career in pictures.

Post continued, stating that Eastwood had changed in the four years since *Hang 'Em High*, especially since becoming his own director.

> We collaborated a lot on that picture, but there were times when he'd come on the set and change the setup or undermine my instructions to one of the actors. Then when the film comes out and makes a lot of money, word goes around that my name was on it, but Clint is the one who really directed. It hurt my career.

Eastwood stated in the biographical "Eastwood: In His Own Words" for the American Film Institute:

> You have to trust your instincts. There's a moment when an actor has it, and he knows it. Behind the camera you can feel the moment even more clearly. And once you've got it, once you feel it, you can't second-guess yourself. If I would go around and ask everyone on the set how it looked, eventually someone would say, "Well, gee, I don't know, there was a fly 600 feet back." Somebody's always going to find a flaw, and pretty soon that flaw gets magnified and you're all back to another take. Meanwhile everyone's forgotten that there's a certain focus on things, and no one's going to see that fly because you're using a 100mm lens. But that's what you can do. You can talk yourself in and out of anything. You can find a million reasons why something didn't work. But if it feels right, and it looks right, it works. Without sounding like a pseudo-intellectual, it's my responsibility to be true to myself. If it works for me, it's right. When I start choosing wrong, I'll step back and let someone else do it for me.

Magnum Force was a potentially interesting look at the dangers of the same vengeful method Callahan had employed. Young rogue cops were taking the law into their own hands by confronting corruption and destroying it without due process. If gangland types managed to avoid a conviction in court, these

Eastwood and Ted Post on the set of *Magnum Force.*

cops gunned them down. They would disrupt drug parties and sex orgies in the same violent manner. Callahan was put in a position to stop what his actions had inspired.

Some believe *Magnum Force* was made in response to those who protested that *Dirty Harry* was a "fascist picture." The film shows the sort of vigilante cops Harry is accused of being; he displays their behaviors as being in contrast to Callahan's approach. Thus, when Harry goes after these cops, he is acting against those who utilize his offbeat methods in a manner that goes against the concept of law enforcement.

But there are problems with *Magnum Force* that have nothing to do with whatever concept was being attempted with the narrative. This was the longest running, and thus most protracted, of the films in which Eastwood reprised the role of Harry Callahan, and it was too disjointed to maintain any strength within its narrative structure. If Post's claims are accurate, and there is no reason to believe otherwise, it may be a case of "too many cooks" causing the movie to lack a firm directorial vision. It appears to be more pessimistic than cynical, more dismissive than guarded. Ted Post does recall one amusing incident:

> Mitchell Ryan, one of the actors in the picture, got sick during filming and couldn't work a couple of days. He had a note sent to me

on the set the day his death scene was supposed to be filmed. The note was from his doctor and it said, "Mitch is too sick to die today."

Eastwood's only 1974 entry was Michael Cimino's *Thunderbolt and Lightfoot*, which attracted Eastwood due to the offbeat characters and the indulgent narrative. Attracted to the cinema of exaggeration, Clint enjoyed this story about a bank robber and a car thief pursuing some buried loot. Eastwood, the screen's great loner, wanted to do a road movie, and although this was an uncharacteristic "buddy pic," it is one of director Cimino's most assured films (his career ranges from the notoriously great *The Deer Hunter* [1978] to the notorious flop *Heaven's Gate* [1980]).

Edward Gallafent stated in his book *Clint Eastwood: Filmmaker and Star*:

> *Thunderbolt and Lightfoot* offers a vision of a post-Korea, post-Vietnam America, a civilization with no redeeming qualities, in which the speed and glamour of the road—the Trans-Am with which the film begins and the Cadillac with which it ends—offer the only moments of pleasure and freedom. Even then, the freedom has no purpose—the couple are caught between an inaccessibly remote past experienced as only violence and loss, a present experienced as dislocation and aversion, and a world without any future that can be formulated.

While Eastwood enjoyed working with Bridges (who received an Oscar nomination as Best Supporting Actor), he was displeased with the way United Artists handled production. He canceled plans for future UA releases from Malpaso and vowed at the time to never work with that studio again.

In 1975 Eastwood was back in the director's chair as well as starring in *The Eiger Sanction*. Eastwood plays a former government assassin who is now living the quiet life of a college art professor, but he is pulled back into his old job to avenge a friend's murder. He also is a highly skilled mountain climber, and this ability ties into the project as well. This Cold War spy thriller emphasizes thrills and danger, but despite taking place in vast open spaces, there is an odd claustrophobic feeling in that the climbers are confined to the mountain, unable to freely move about. *The Eiger Sanction* was a very dangerous shoot, where the actors risked their lives, and at least one (body double David Knowles) was killed during a rock fall. Taut, thrilling, and suspenseful, *The Eiger Sanction* was still only an average film, and beneath the talents of Eastwood and supporting actor George Kennedy, who had also been in *Thunderbolt and Lightfoot*.

Eastwood told Roger Ebert in an interview:

> I didn't want to use a stunt man, because I wanted to use a telephoto lens and zoom in slowly all the way to my face—so you could see it was really me. I put on a little disguise and slipped into a sneak pre-

view of the film to see how people liked it. When I was hanging up there in the air, the woman in front of me said to her friend, "Gee, I wonder how they did that?" and her friend said, "Special effects."

The Eiger Sanction received bad reviews from the critics and was a box office disappointment. Eastwood felt the studio's lack of enthusiasm for the project resulted in poor publicity and limited box office.

Each of these non-westerns made after *High Plains Drifter* (1973) continued to use elements like vigilantism, isolationism, and stoicism; Eastwood continued to be inspired by his past work as his talents as an actor and filmmaker expanded. Even the uncharacteristic buddy movie *Thunderbolt and Lightfoot* seemed more like an extension of the hapless partners Eastwood had in his Harry Callahan films, or the unlikely allegiance he made at the conclusion of *Two Mules for Sister Sara* (1970). While many critics at the time felt he was too stiff in his performances, Eastwood was smart enough to realize that the character he had created, and allowed to evolve, was most effective when he did or said little.

Upon completion of *The Eiger Sanction*, Clint Eastwood's contract with Universal Studios was now up. Eastwood had become unhappy with the studio and chose not to renew with the studio and investigated opportunities elsewhere. He contacted Frank Wells at Warner Bros., who, according to Schickel's biography, had been making overtures to the actor-filmmaker for some time. Eastwood inquired as to Warner Bros.' interest in his making his films for that studio. Frank Wells indicated the studio would be quite pleased to have Clint Eastwood make his films for them. Eastwood then told Wells an idea he had for a new western.

CHAPTER 14

The Outlaw Josey Wales (1976)

(A Malpaso film released through Warner Bros.)
Director: Clint Eastwood
Screenplay: Philip Kaufman, Sonia Chernus; from the book *The Rebel Outlaw Josey Wales*, later retitled *Gone to Texas*, by Forrest Carter (aka Asa Earl Carter)
Producer: Robert Daley
Associate Producers: James Fargo, John G. Wilson
Music: Jerry Fielding
Cinematography: Bruce Surtees
Editing: Ferris Webster
Cast: Clint Eastwood (Josey Wales), Chief Dan George (Lone Watie), Sondra Locke (Laura Lee), Bill McKinney (Terrill), John Vernon (Fletcher), Paula Trueman (Grandma Sarah), Sam Bottoms (Jamie), Geraldine Kearns (Little Moonlight), Woodrow Parfrey (Carpetbagger), Joyce Jameson (Rose), Sheb Wooley (Travis Cobb), Royal Dano (Ten Spot), Matt Clarke (Kelly), John Verros (Chato), Will Sampson (Ten Bears), William O'Connell (Sim Carstairs), Kyle Eastwood (Josey's Son), Cissy Wellman (Josey's Wife), John Quade (Comanchero Leader), Richard Farnsworth (Comanchero), Danny Green (Lemuel), Madeleine Taylor Holmes (Grannie Hawkins), Faye Hamblin (Grandpa), Erik Holland (Union Army Sergeant), Frank Scho-field (Senator Lane), Buck Kartalian (Shopkeeper), Len Lesser (Abe), Doug McGrath (Lige), John Russell (Bloody Bill Anderson), Charles Tyner (Zukie Limmer), Bruce M. Fischer (Yoke), John Mitchum (Al), John Chandler, (1st Bounty Hunter), Tom Roy Lowe (2nd Bounty Hunter), Clay Tanner (1st Texas Ranger), Robert F. Hoy (2nd Texas Ranger), Frank Cockrell (Soldier), Walter Scott (Drunk).
Budget: $3,700,000 (estimated)
Gross: $31,800,000 (USA)
Release Date: June 30, 1976
Running Time: 135 minutes

Sound Mix: Mono
Color: Technicolor
Aspect Ratio: 2.35: 1
Availability: DVD and Blu-ray (Warner Home Video)

The Outlaw Josey Wales is Clint Eastwood's fifth self-directed feature, and the film is the second western for which he acted as director. It is also his best-directed film to date, offering the culmination of his being influenced by Leone and Siegel, resulting in his own vision. However, *The Outlaw Josey Wales*, while a consistently brilliant western, was fraught with problems regarding its conception, its execution, and its aftermath.

Eastwood was initially attracted to a poorly printed booklet titled *The Rebel Outlaw: Josey Wales* by Forrest Carter when it was given to him by producer Bob Daley. It was one of many items that came flooding into the Malpaso offices. Usually these unsolicited manuscripts are quickly returned unread, but the cover letter accompanying this story intrigued Daley. It referred to Eastwood's "kind eyes," and humbly hoped they would look upon the offering with some consideration. Daley was completely absorbed by the story and gave it to Eastwood to read. The actor agreed with his producer, and arrangements were made to secure the movie rights for Malpaso.

Poster for *The Outlaw Josey Wales.*

During the waning days of the Civil War, Josey Wales (Eastwood) is a simple farmer whose wife and son are murdered by Senator James Lane's Union jayhawkers. He buries his family and joins a group of Confederate soldiers, seeking revenge. When the war ends, Josey refuses to surrender to the Union forces, led by Captain Fletcher (John Vernon), who promise amnesty to the Confederate soldiers. Captain Terrill (Bill McKinney) orders the massacre of the Confederates who have surrendered. Josey intervenes during the massacre, in which he blows away several Union Redlegs with a Gatling gun. He teams for a while with Jamie (Sam Bottoms), a recalcitrant young man and the only other survivor of the massacre, but he soon dies from injuries sustained in the attack. Josey then sets out as a loner, still bent on revenge. He becomes a wanted man, with a $5,000 reward for his capture, dead or alive. Pursued by bounty hunters as well as Union soldiers, Josey puts together a group of diverse companions that include an elderly Cherokee (Chief Dan George), a Navajo woman (Geraldine Keams), an older white lady (Paula Trueman), and her young adult granddaughter (Sondra Locke).

Eastwood drew from his own screen persona for much of the Josey Wales character—his vigilantism, his semi-loner status, his defiance of authority and setting his own rules—while offering a vulnerability and a purpose that is more immediate than what his previous western characters had experienced. Josey Wales and his family live in Missouri, a state that remained neutral throughout the Civil War. It's likely that prior to the murder of his family, Josey had no preference toward either the Union or the Confederacy; any interest or involvement he has in the war is purely out of his thirst for vengeance.

Eastwood offers an establishing scene of Wales farming his land, with his son (real-life son Kyle Eastwood) accompanying him. The child is called in the house, and soon noise from afar alerts Josey who runs toward his home to find it aflame, surrounded by Union attackers. He attempts to stop the men as they carry his screaming, flailing wife (Cissy Wellman) from the home, but he is hit over the head. Eastwood chooses to shoot this from the perspective of the man, on horseback, who hits him, presenting Josey from an elevated camera shot. The blow strikes, and Josey falls to the ground. The next shot fades in to him burying his family.

In one of the most emotionally striking moments of the film's early scenes, Josey is shown dragging a wrapped corpse to a hole he has dug. As he drags the lifeless body, a hand slips out of the wrapping. Eastwood shoots this in close-up, as Josey's own hand comes into the frame and gently tucks the dead body's hand back into the wrapping. It is presumably his son, as the hand is badly burned. Once the bodies are buried, Josey clutches the wooden cross he has placed as a marker on one of the graves, succumbs to emotion, and cries hard as he leans on, and bends, the cross to make it look similar to the cross on the Confederate battle flag. The raw emotion Eastwood allows his character to exhibit is much different than the stoicism exhibited in his other movies (and throughout the rest of this one). But it helps to clarify the impact of the motivation that inspires his actions for the duration of the narrative.

Eastwood's cinematic structure is already quite evident at this point in the film. The tranquil opening scenes suddenly cut to the fiery attack on Josey's home, upending his life swiftly and brutally. The farmer's life appears quiet and simple. He is forced to run into the action. The attack is random.

Josey then finds a pair of pistols that were unharmed by the fire, and he proceeds to learn to shoot until he can do so quickly and accurately. Unlike Eastwood's other loner characters, Josey does not enter the scene already possessing these skills. It is obvious that prior to this he lived a peaceful, average life, and we get to see the motivation he has for becoming a vigilante.

Eastwood said in an interview with Patrick McGilligan in 1976 that *The Outlaw Josey Wales* is "a saga. It's about the character I play, whereas in *The Good, the Bad and the Ugly* the only character you got to know—somewhat—is the Eli Wallach character. In other words, Josey Wales is a hero, and you see how he gets to where he is—rather than just having a mysterious hero appear on the plains and become involved with other people's plights."

The film also includes another of Eastwood's favorite character dynamics—the principal character being paired with an unlikely partner (however, not for very long). He and Jamie connect, despite initial conflict, but this character dies fairly early in the narrative, and nothing substantial is developed in their relationship. What this character dynamic does convey is his connection to outcasts, having become one himself. It sets up the band of outcasts he compiles, from the two Native Americans to the two white women whom Josey saves from an attack by Native Americans. Unlike the more conventional westerns, *The Outlaw Josey Wales* offers more than one perspective and does not settle on stereotyping.

While flowing seamlessly from narrative exposition to action sequence, Eastwood utilizes the close-ups and quick edits that sustained the work of his mentors. He also makes great use of the beautiful scenery, especially in the establishing shots, where Eastwood makes use of the wide-screen image by framing the characters in the brightness and colors of the negative space by which they're surrounded.

Josey finally meets up with Terrill when the Redlegs attack him and his group as they are holed up in a fortified ranch house, which allows the outcasts to overpower the guerilla forces. Josey pursues Terrill on horseback as the captain tries to escape. Josey is out of ammunition, but he points his unloaded pistols in Terrill's face and fires all empty chambers at him. Terrill does little during this, being psychologically overtaken by the action, and not certain each chamber is empty. When he attacks Josey with his cavalry sword, it is Terrill who is stabbed to death with his own weapon.

While the killing of Terrill is Josey's ultimate revenge, there are several elements that offer another kind of vengeance. Josey was powerless in rescuing his wife and child from death. The narrative allows him to successfully rescue women on his trails. First it is the Navajo woman, Little Moonlight (Keams), who is about to be raped by hillbillies, who recognize Wales and believe they can capture him for the bounty. He effortlessly blows them away in the same manner as his western characters had done since his Leone films. The next instance occurs when the grandmother and granddaughter are rescued from an Indian attack where the men have already been killed.

In the film's conclusion, Josey, wounded from his battle with Terrill, enters a saloon and finds two Texas rangers, along with Captain Fletcher. The locals refer to Josey as "Wilson" and insist Josey Wales was killed during a shootout in Mexico. The rangers accept this and move on. Fletcher, however, recognizes Josey. Seeing that he is wounded, Fletcher states that he will give Wales "the first move" because "I owe you that." Josey states, "we all died a little during the war," and rides off.

The way Eastwood shoots this final scene is another of the clear examples of his directorial vision. The saloon scene is framed in darkness, with the locals and the rangers in the foreground, while Fletcher lurks in the background. It is so dark in this area of the saloon that the brim of Fletcher's hat shades his face. His identity is revealed when he lifts his head, and his eyes are visible from the window light. Josey recognizes him. So does the viewer. This clever revealing shot is one of the most impressive in the film.

Eastwood uses darkness effectively elsewhere in the film. Many indoor scenes are bathed in darkness, including when a bounty hunter finds Josey and prepares to take him in, dead or alive, for the reward. It is this scene in which the man indicates being a bounty hunter is his living, causing the classic reply, "Dyin' ain't much of a livin'." The man is quickly blown away by Wales.

Eastwood's visuals carry the rhythm of the narrative so that its long running time never seems protracted. He never holds his shots for very long, and when Josey is engaged in a confrontation where spectators are nearby, quick cutaways to close-up shots of their faces go by in seconds, which is just enough to offer their reactions. Techniques like these help break up each scene, strengthening the narrative structure. Scott McGee stated for Turner Classic Movies:

> While *High Plains Drifter* was bleak and symbolic, *The Outlaw Josey Wales*—the film and the character—is a man at war with himself, one who doubts his humanity, mourns his past, and kills the hated.

Eastwood replaces Josey's inability to rescue his wife by rescuing other women, all of whom become attached to him at different levels. The Navajo considers herself his property. The granddaughter is attracted to his rugged heroism. The grandmother establishes herself as group matriarch but looks up to him as the leader of the disparate group.

Perhaps the most interesting character in this group is the elder Native American, played by Chief Dan George, only a few years after his star-making role in Arthur Penn's *Little Big Man* (1970). George, who was, like Eastwood, a commanding presence with little expression, is the anchor of each scene in which he appears. He and Josey have a reversal of the father-son relationship that Wales lost with the death of his child, and again when Jamie dies of his injuries. In Richard Schickel's biography of Eastwood, Clint admitted to being in tears when he and the Indian actor were "saying what they both imagine is a final farewell." Schickel quoted Eastwood as saying, "I thought, God, how am I going to keep my composure if he is going to tug at me like that?" Chief Dan George often had trouble remembering his lines as they were written in the script, so Eastwood would instead direct him to tell a story he knew, and George was so good at this, his lines fit comfortably into the scenario.

The portrayal of Native Americans in this film sets it apart from other westerns that had been made up to that point. Even though there are Indian attacks alluded to in the story, they are not just a nameless, villainous force, and a couple of them become the hero's allies and are given unique personalities.

As the granddaughter, Sondra Locke was making her first appearance in a Clint Eastwood film. She would soon become quite a significant person in Eastwood's life, and she would appear in more of his movies. At the time, she was best known for having scored as the young tomboy in Robert Ellis Miller's *The Heart Is a Lonely Hunter* (1968), but she had done mostly television before appearing in *The Outlaw Josey Wales*. A small five feet, four inches, weighing barely 100 pounds, her diminutive frailty offered what was necessary for the character. Locke recalled in Schickel's book that Eastwood's interest in realism included an emphasis on her using very little makeup.

Eastwood originally wanted one of the film's screenwriters, Philip Kaufman, to direct *The Outlaw Josey Wales*, having been impressed with his directorial work on the western *The Great Northfield Minnesota Raid* (1972). Kaufman completed pre-production work, but when production began, his approach conflicted with Eastwood's method. Kaufman liked to ponder what to do while Eastwood liked to come on the set and start shooting. Kaufman would insist on more takes than Eastwood felt necessary on a scene. When the actor would ask what he should do differently, the director would say to do it the same way, he just felt repetition would make the scene deeper. This was counter to the way the impatient Eastwood liked to do things. Arrangements were then made for producer Daley to fire Kaufman from the project. This caused a problem with the Director's Guild, as all pre-production (choosing a location, hiring actors, having sets built, and so on) had been completed. Eastwood refused to back down to the Guild, as did Warner Bros., resulting in new legislation being passed. The Director's Guild created the "Clint Eastwood Rule," which stated that a major fine could be imposed on a production when a director is discharged and replaced by the person who discharged the director.

Forrest Carter, writer of the original story, was another problem. After securing him an agent and arranging for the book to be published by a leading press (under the title *Gone to Texas*), producer Daley had Carter flown in to Hollywood to discuss the project and secure the rights. When the writer showed up, he was drunk. His behaviors included urinating on the carpeting of the Satellite Lounge, and holding a knife to the throat of a Malpaso secretary during a dinner meeting, proclaiming his love for her and threatening to kill her if she did not reciprocate. The producers realized they were dealing with a sociopath, and it is for these reasons he was kept away from the production. However, once the movie was released, it was discovered that Carter was also connected with the Ku Klux Klan and had allegedly written Alabama governor George Wallace's noted "segregation now, segregation tomorrow, segregation forever," quote (he would later break from Wallace when the governor changed his attitude about segregation). While these revelations did not harm the movie's box office, they were widely reported, causing Eastwood, Malpaso, and Warner Bros. to completely distance themselves from any further work from this author. Carter died three years later.

The Outlaw Josey Wales became one of Eastwood's most profitable films, and the film remains among his most beloved. In his review for the *Chicago Sun Times*, Roger Ebert stated:

> Clint Eastwood's *The Outlaw Josey Wales* is a strange and daring Western that brings together two of the genre's usually incompatible story lines. On the one hand, it's about a loner, a man of action and few words, who turns his back on civilization and lights out for the Indian nations. On the other hand, it's about a group of people heading West who meet along the trail and cast their destinies together. What happens next is supposed to be against the rules in Westerns, as if *Jeremiah Johnson* were crossed with *Stagecoach*: Eastwood, the loner, becomes the group's leader and father figure. Eastwood plays essentially the same character he's been developing since the Dollar Westerns. He says little, keeps his face in the shadows, has an almost godlike personal invulnerability, and lives by a code we have to intuit because he'd die rather than explain it aloud. Various, and inexhaustible, bounty hunters are constantly on the outlaw's trail, despite the Eastwood ability (in this movie as before) to wipe out six, eight, ten bad guys before they can get off a shot. Eastwood is such a taciturn

and action-oriented performer that it's easy to overlook the fact that he directs many of his movies—and many of the best, most intelligent ones. Here, with the moody, gloomily beautiful, photography of Bruce Surtees, he creates a magnificent Western feeling.

The Outlaw Josey Wales was enormously popular with moviegoers. *Variety*, however, was less enthusiastic, stating:

> The screenplay is another one of those violence revues, with carnage production numbers slotted every so often and intercut with Greek chorus narratives by John Vernon and Chief Dan George.

Dave Kehr, in the *Chicago Reader* said that the film

> shows an almost equal balance between his two main influences, Sergio Leone and Don Siegel. As the title character, a Confederate guerrilla out to avenge the murder of his family by Union redlegs, Eastwood combines the cold pragmatism of a Leone hero with the strident Old Testament morality of a Siegel protagonist. Although the last part of the film becomes repetitive and slightly confused, Eastwood manages the picaresque plot with skill, and his visuals have a high-charged, almost Germanic quality. Wales also possesses a touching emotional vulnerability that marks another significant step away from Eastwood's often-overcriticized "macho" image.

Despite mixed reviews, *The Outlaw Josey Wales* received unsolicited testimonial comments from celebrities of the day. Johnny Carson, popular host of NBC television's *The Tonight Show*, promoted the film on TV by calling it "the greatest western of all time." Filmmaker Orson Welles, during a 1982 guest appearance on *The Merv Griffin Show*, stated: "When I saw *The Outlaw Josey Wales* for the fourth time, I realized that it belongs with the great Westerns. You know, the great Westerns of Ford and Hawks and people like that." The interest and appreciation of this film continues, and is always mentioned in interviews, essays, and articles on Clint Eastwood. As late as 2010, David Denby stated in reference to this film in the *Telegraph*:

> If Leone emptied the West in his early movies, making Westerns that were mainly syntax and dead bodies, Eastwood, working in long paragraphs, put meaning back into the genre. Landscape as moral destiny, a miscellaneous community as the American way—these were the first signs in Eastwood of both a wider social sympathy and an incipient distaste for the conventions of genre plotting.

This would be the first of six films in which Sondra Locke would co-star with Eastwood, due to a relationship that began during the filming of *The*

Outlaw Josey Wales. And while Eastwood remained married to his wife Maggie Johnson until 1984 (they were legally separated in 1978 after a period of estrangement), he and Locke would be in a relationship from 1975 until 1989 (during which Locke would remain married to her much older, and openly gay, husband, Gordon Anderson).[1] Eastwood was friendly with Anderson, and he even purchased a house for him and his male companion. While their screen pairings were often quite fruitful, especially as Eastwood continued experimenting with different ideas and approaches, his and Locke's bitter breakup would make headlines.

Clint Eastwood's success was so assured by this point that he once again decided to investigate other possibilities in film. While he made another sequel to *Dirty Harry*, some of Eastwood's choices extended not only to different genres, but roles that were as far from Harry Callahan, Joe, Manco, Blondie, or Josey Wales as his creative interest would reach.

Eastwood finished off the wildly successful decade of the 1970s by not only taking chances as an actor, but also as a director. He only directed one more movie during the balance of this decade, but it turned out to be one of his most courageous and misunderstood. As the 1970s concluded, Eastwood would also appear in what would become the most financially successful film of his career, as well as his most offbeat. These odd-yet-successful choices further solidified his status one of America's strongest and most durable motion picture stars.

When Clint Eastwood does return to the western genre at the top of the following decade, it is with an offbeat entry in the genre and yet another in our study that does not rest as comfortably in being defined within the western genre. But the film *Bronco Billy* (1980) comes along after a series of offbeat, successful films that redefine his screen persona and extend past its parameters into different ideas. It continues to demonstrate that all of Clint Eastwood's movies are informed by his westerns, and that the films that he makes within that genre continue to extend beyond conventional parameters.

Note

1. It was also revealed in 1989 that Eastwood fathered a child, Kimber, with a dancer, Roxanne Tunis, in 1964.

CHAPTER 15

Between the Westerns (1976–1979)

By the mid-1970s, Clint Eastwood had secured a level of top movie stardom, which further increased his supervisory control over his projects. This also led to some interesting choices as this successful decade concluded. Eastwood finished off the 1970s by venturing further away from the conventional character elements that established his work.

Upon finishing *The Outlaw Josey Wales* (1976), Eastwood made another sequel to *Dirty Harry* with first-time director James Fargo, a former assistant director on a few of Eastwood's other films. However, while *Magnum Force* (1973) was a letdown from the original *Dirty Harry* (1971), this next one, *The Enforcer* (1976), showed the series lapsing into tepid formula. Perhaps there was some element of topical humor to pair cantankerous Harry with a liberated female partner (Tyne Daly), but the film then rests on stereotypes and predictable situations. Entertaining in the most superficial manner, it lacked the strength of the first film even more so than its immediate predecessor. The only real strength behind *The Enforcer* is Eastwood's recognizing the possibilities for comic satire with his character. The stoic Harry is often presented as bemused or befuddled—traits that were either subdued or nonexistent in earlier portrayals of the character. *The Enforcer* rests a bit too heavily on the externals of Harry's character (his wry sarcasm, no-nonsense approach, macho posturing) without any real substance.

Harry Callahan evolved in similar ways as Eastwood's western antihero did, only with not so successful results. Both began as loners with their own agenda. But in Eastwood's westerns, the pairing of his character with others created an interesting dynamic without diverting too far from the character's original traits (*Two Mules for Sister Sara* [1970], *The Outlaw Josey Wales*, among others), while in the Dirty Harry series, Harry isn't a consistent character, and pairing him up

Eastwood appeared as Harry Callahan for the third time in *The Enforcer*.

with someone else comes off as less of an attempt at character development and more as an isolated novelty. *The Enforcer* is comical and conventional.

The only real positive aspect of *The Enforcer* is how its perspective informed *The Gauntlet* (1977), which is the next film Eastwood directed himself. Long vilified by the more literal-minded moviegoer, *The Gauntlet* is actually one of Eastwood's most interesting and courageous movies. He plays a cop who is as far removed from Harry Callahan as can be—drunken, unreliable, and dispensable. His defiance and detachment is not due to a superior attitude with skills to back it up. It is because he wallows in abject self-loathing and simply doesn't care. This cop must escort a key witness (Sondra Locke) across the country while both the mob, and the police force, pursue him (there is a tangential connection within the narrative). On more than one occasion, he is holed up in a secluded area (a bus, a cottage) while seemingly hundreds of his pursuers surround the area and open fire. The structure is demolished, but somehow, both he and his prisoner manage to survive.

The cop Eastwood plays in *The Gauntlet* is not defiant of authority, is not a maverick, and has always been a company man. But he is old, tired, used up, and considered expendable by the nefarious powers-that-be. With enough star clout to take a big chance, Eastwood made a film that challenged his image and stretched all manner of credibility. Its breakneck pace and violent action keeps it entertaining. Clint only fires his gun twice in the entire movie (he uses it to threaten people at gunpoint several times), and he spends most of the movie being shot at and escaping impossible situations.

The Gauntlet was Clint Eastwood's most expensive film to date, with a $5 million budget. Initially it was considered as a possible co-starring film with Barbra Streisand playing opposite him, but Eastwood grew impatient with her hesitation about taking the part and cast Locke. The film was a financial success, with a total domestic gross of over $26 million, proving that the box office clout of Eastwood's name did not need another star like Streisand to ensure ticket sales. However, the outrageousness of the situations, the pat ending, and Eastwood's playing a loser rather than a winner resulted in moviegoers exhibiting continued disdain for this effort. Eastwood told Roger Ebert in a *Chicago Sun Times* interview that he realized some of his more offbeat artistic decisions would not net the same response from his following as the films in which he offered a more familiar, conventional version of his screen persona. And while films like *The Gauntlet* did net a profit, it was not at the same level as other films (e.g., *The Enforcer* grossed $20 million more than *The Gauntlet* had). It would not be the last time Eastwood worked against type, and it is this film that was most instrumental at inspiring his next venture into the western genre a few years later.

Perhaps the most significant film made during this period of his career is the cornball comedy *Every Which Way but Loose* (1978), in which he played a street fighter who pals around with a pet orangutan. Burt Reynolds had hit it big with the country comedy *Smokey and the Bandit* (1976), so scripts of that nature were floating around Hollywood during this period. Films featuring a fighter were also popular, with two Sylvester Stallone movies—*Rocky* (1976) and *Paradise Alley* (1978), the latter about wrestling—inspiring other movies like *The One and Only* (1978), *The Main Event* (1979), *The Prize Fighter* (1979), and even Martin Scorsese's *Raging Bull* (1980).

Comedies for rural demographics became nationwide hits during the 1950s with the Ma and Pa Kettle series while Eastwood was working for the same studio, Universal. They also enjoyed popularity in the 1960s on television with shows like *The Beverly Hillbillies, Petticoat Junction, Green Acres,* and *The Andy Griffith Show.* Even an Elvis Presley vehicle, *Kissin' Cousins* (1964), responded to this subgenre's popularity at the time, becoming yet another moneymaker for the singer.

Eastwood was interested in doing a straight comedy; he ignored the fact that nearly every one of his associates tried to talk him out of it. They felt the script's unbridled silliness would tarnish his image. Despite its having been a box office hit, *The Gauntlet* was generating word-of-mouth that viewers didn't want to see Eastwood in this sort of part too frequently, and preferred he keep making movies that traded off his established persona. Eastwood realized the script for *Every Which Way but Loose* allowed him to do that, as the central character is a no-nonsense street fighter with many of the same traits as his most popular western or detective roles. The script was by no means a witty comedy; it was instead the sort of cornball comic silliness that one would find in the aforementioned Elvis Presley movie. Continuing to be an actor who took chances, Eastwood hired James Fargo to direct and went ahead with the project, despite the misgivings of his staff.

Every Which Way but Loose was not only Clint Eastwood's most financially successful movie, it was the second highest grossing film that year (the first was the blockbuster *Superman*). Critics were dismissive, calling the film "junk" (Rona Barrett went so far as to state that Eastwood owed his fans an apology for having made it). The critics had no impact on moviegoers. Audiences of all ages responded to the lightweight nonsense in a most positive manner. Its domestic gross was over $50 million, which was ten times its production costs. Sondra Locke co-starred (and sang a duet with Phil Everly of the Everly Brothers), as did frequent Eastwood supporting actor Geoffrey Lewis, and veteran actress-writer Ruth Gordon (who, with her husband Garson Kanin, co-wrote several witty Spencer Tracy–Katharine Hepburn films, but who was now making a career playing eccentric old ladies). Eastwood believes theaters in the southern states and middle America were responsible for the movie's massive success, stating for Richard Schickel, "[T]hey'd go to see it, and then keep coming back to see it again—it would play for weeks and weeks." While not a western, *Every Which Way but Loose* has ties to the western genre. It takes place in somewhat of a western setting, and Eastwood's character is a sort of modern cowboy, roaming from place to place searching for adventure.

Clint followed up this hit with one of the best non-western films of his career. *Escape from Alcatraz* (1979), a prison drama, was to be his final film with Don Siegel at the helm. The relationship between the two was, at this point, a bit strained from a professional perspective. *Dirty Harry* had made Eastwood a superstar and Siegel an A-list director. As Clint himself began achieving success as a director, there was a certain competitive spirit (especially with Eastwood's penchant for taking over direction on his films, which led to animosity with both Ted Post and James Fargo, neither of whom worked with him again). The script for *Escape from Alcatraz* was being shopped around the studios with Siegel already attached as director. Because of Siegel's track record, including the success of his *Riot in Cell Block 11* (1954), producers were immediately interested in supporting this project. Siegel likely felt he did not need Eastwood, nor did Eastwood believe he needed Siegel, but both responded to the prospect of success if they worked together on this project. Paramount Pictures's head of production, Michael Eisner, was instrumental in putting the two men together.

Escape from Alcatraz is based on the true story of the highly intelligent Frank Morris (who had an IQ in the neighborhood of 140) and his notorious escape from a prison that was deemed inescapable. The narrative maintains how Morris (Eastwood) and a group of carefully selected comrades slowly and cleverly figure a way of escaping the impenetrable prison while developing each character individually and also presenting the ugly aspects of prison life. Morris must fend off a sexually attracted prisoner who is twice his size (Bruce Fischer), sees a sensitive artist (Roberts Blossom) driven to madness when his painting privileges are removed by a sadistic warden (Patrick McGoohan), and contends with the humiliating treatment of solitary confinement. Using a film noir approach, Siegel would later call *Escape from Alcatraz* a black-and-white movie that happened to be shot in color. *Escape from Alcatraz* was another box office success, and the film also garnered Eastwood the best reviews of his career thus far. Frank Rich in *Time* noted Siegel's vision via the cinematography and also stated, "At a time when Hollywood entertainments are more overblown than ever, Eastwood proves that less really is more." In an era of blockbusters like *Star Wars* (1977) and *Superman* (1978), a straight drama like *Escape from Alcatraz* was passionately welcomed by critics and more serious moviegoers, while also spilling over into success with mainstream moviegoers.

This film also had a far reaching effect on Eastwood's later screen work. His most successful films during the latter half of his career, particularly the ones he made in the 1990s, are very character driven. Films like *Million Dollar Baby* (2004) and *Gran Torino* (2008), for example, are less about the action and more about the people and their relationships.

As a new decade dawned, Clint Eastwood was enjoying ever-increasing stardom and believed that the enormous box office numbers of the offbeat *Every Which Way but Loose* indicated he could enjoy success with different approaches to the film genres in which he frequently worked, and his screen persona. Eastwood had been challenging the conventions of the Hollywood western since Sergio Leone's Dollars trilogy, but from that point, most of his performances in the genre offered some consistent similarities with the character. However, Eastwood's next western was his most offbeat one in this genre.

In *Bronco Billy* (1980), Eastwood explored the cowboy outside his comfortable trappings much as he had in *Coogan's Bluff* (1968). But instead of trying to find his way within the parameters of a big city, the title character in *Bronco Billy* was a cowboy whose response to the modern world was to run a Wild West show. Not the confident revisionist approach to the conventional cowboy hero, the character in *Bronco Billy* had Eastwood playing another loser—a struggling performer whose ideas and future plans remain fixed on an existence that offers little in the way of success.

More than challenging the western genre, his established screen persona, or exploring more deeply as a director, *Bronco Billy* was to become a film that Clint Eastwood would continue to remember with fondness. Responding to a happy set, a story that interested him, and the chance to play another character that ventured away from his established screen persona, *Bronco Billy* was a film that completely satisfied its director and star. For the remainder of his career, *Bronco Billy* would consistently be referred to as a film that Eastwood fondly recalled.

CHAPTER 16

Bronco Billy (1980)

(Produced by Warner Bros. in association with Second Street Films)[1]
Director: Clint Eastwood
Screenplay: Dennis Hackin
Producers: Neal H. Dobrofsky, Dennis Hackin
Executive Producer: Robert Daley
Associate Producer: Fritz Manes
Cinematography: David Worth
Editing: Joel Cox, Ferris Webster
Cast: Clint Eastwood (Bronco Billy); Sondra Locke (Antoinette Lily); Geoffrey
    Lewis (John Arlington); Scatman Crothers (Doc Lynch); Bill McKinney
    (Lefty LeBow); Sam Bottoms (Leonard James); Dan Vadis (Chief Big
    Eagle); Sierra Pecheur (Lorraine Running Water); Walter Barnes (Sheriff
    Dix); Woodrow Parfrey (Dr. Canterbury); Beverlee McKinsey (Irene Lily);
    Doug McGrath (Lt. Wiecker); George Wendt (Bartender); Hank Worden
    (Station Mechanic); William Prince (Edgar Lipton); Tessa Richarde (Mitzi
    Fritts); Tanya Russell (Doris Duke); Valerie Shanks (Sister Maria); Pam
    Abbas (Mother Superior); Eyde Byrde (Eloise); Douglas Copsey, Danny
    Jensen (Reporters); Arlis Tranmer (Photographer); John Wesley Elliot Jr.
    (Sanatorium Attendant); Chuck Hicks, Robert F. Hoy, George Orrison
    (Cowboys at Bar); Jefferson Jewell (Boy at Bank); Dawneen Lee (Bank
    Teller); Don Mummert (Chauffeur); Lloyd Nelson (Sanatorium Police-
    man); Michael Reinbold (King); James Simmerman (Bank Manager);
    Roger Dale Simmons, Jenny Sternling (Reporters); Chuck Waters, Jerry
    Wills (Bank Robbers); Alison Eastwood, Kyle Eastwood (Orphans); Merle
    Haggard (Himself).
Budget: $5.5 million
Gross: $24,265,659
Release Date: June 11, 1980
Running Time: 116 minutes
Sound Mix: Mono
Color: Technicolor
Aspect Ratio: 1.85: 1
Availability: DVD (Warner Home Video)

As they became too old for their movie careers, a lot of actors in B-movie westerns joined traveling Wild West shows, where they would set up in a small town and offer performances of skills that were no longer needed in the movies (trick riding, roping, stunts, and such). In the title role of Bronco Billy McCoy, Clint Eastwood plays a cowboy without a movie career as his backstory, just one whose skills only thrive within the context of such shows. He runs his own, calling it Bronco Billy's Wild West Show, but with little success. Traveling with a band of various small-time performers, they go from town to town and make so little money, the acts have not been paid in weeks. The story takes a turn when a runaway heiress (Sondra Locke) ends up traveling with them, taking the spot of Billy's female accomplice who has balloons shot from around her by a blindfolded Billy as she is strapped to a rotating target.

When Eastwood and Locke made *The Gauntlet* (1977), some reviewers noticed a tangential similarity to Frank Capra's *It Happened One Night* (1934), with its story of an unlikely couple traveling cross-country while being pursued. In *Bronco Billy*, that idea is generated again, with Locke playing an heiress who is running from her own circumstances (as Claudette Colbert had in the Capra film). Eastwood is hardly the crusading reporter with an ulterior motive that Clark Gable had been in the earlier film, but he does find the haughty heiress a refreshing-if-annoying addition to the troupe, especially when she agrees to perform in a role that he has had trouble casting.

Eastwood's direction immediately calls attention to the show's lack of popularity with the opening scene. Scatman Crothers plays a happy host to a small smattering of spectators who dot the bleachers while performances such as a snake-handling Indian (who gets bit by poisonous snakes) and Billy's own trick riding offer them some level of entertainment. This is obviously the seamier side of the popular live rodeo, a small-scale traveling show that survives on almost no money. When the acts mention not having been paid, Billy takes umbrage and they back down, offering the idea that they would rather be part of something for no pay than alone in the world. This sort of camaraderie continues, even when the heiress appears and disrupts the proceedings with her superior attitude.

It can be argued that the film plays on stereotypes, which is true to the extent that Eastwood is playing this film for comedy. It is not the sort of rural comedy *Every Which Way but Loose* (1978) had been, however. Eastwood, upon reading the script, recognized the Capra influence and was trying to make a comedy in that manner. He succeeds to some extent. But, unlike Capra, Eastwood does not have several strong characters right down to the smallest bit. He has a likeable cast of supporting actors while he and Sondra Locke carry the narrative. The ending might seem a bit pat (Locke's character returns to her lavish lifestyle after suffering through the limitations of the show's lack of funds, but is bored and returns to the show), but it is an effective conclusion to the proceedings,

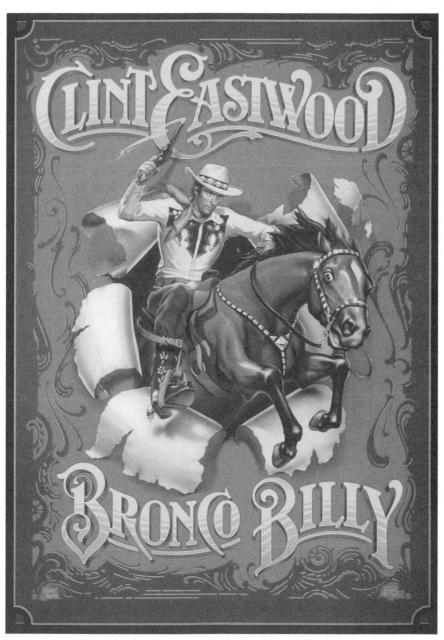

Poster for *Bronco Billy*.

which includes a brief time where the missing heiress is listed as having died (her fiancé plans to abscond with her money).

The film's $5 million budget resulted in a profit, but not one as substantial as Eastwood had hoped, despite a strong opening weekend. Critics liked the movie—Janet Maslin called it "the best and funniest Clint Eastwood movie in quite a while"—but audiences did not like Eastwood to venture too far away from his established persona for too long (other actors who established strong screen characters had the same problem with their fans, including Eastwood's idol James Cagney).

Eastwood had turned fifty, and some critics felt he was mellowing his screen character a bit as a result. Eastwood told interviewer John Vinocur:

> America is the maddest idea in the world, put together by madmen. So here comes this tent with its collage of crazies. I wanted to say something about everybody being able to participate.

So Bronco Billy is presented as a folksy character who addresses the children in his audience with "finish your oatmeal, do what your ma and pa tell you, don't ever tell a lie, say your prayers," and other such advice. This is not so much the actor mellowing as the character being presented as the sort of small-time ersatz hero who has been inspired by the more noted movie cowboys of yore (Roy Rogers, et al.), whose skills and impact were at a greater level, and who addressed children with the same values.

In *Clint Eastwood: Filmmaker and Star*, Edward Gallafent states:

> I believe that the film makes two claims regarding this world of pieties. First, that in the contemporary world they can exist only in this space, an America contained inside a bizarre iconography of patriotism. Second, that they are the values that this—in interviews Eastwood described him as a "naive messiah"—has chosen to give to the creature of his invention. That Billy can articulate them is part of his naivety, which runs right through the film.

Eastwood was fascinated by this character study, perhaps much more than he was by the Capraesque plot, and would continue to recall the affability among the actors and crew during the shooting of the film. Eastwood told Vinocur:

> It was an old fashioned theme, probably too old fashioned as the film didn't do as well as we hoped. But if, as a film director, I ever wanted to say something you'll find it in *Bronco Billy*.

What Eastwood seemed to be going for is a balance between the old west and how someone with these same attitudes survived in the modern world. Bronco

Billy survives by creating his own niche, where his archaic performance skills fit in well, despite limited financial success.

The heiress character works against type within the trappings of what seems like a stereotypical role. While sufficiently haughty and condescending, the heiress is also capable with a gun, matching Billy's sharpshooting skills and greatly impressing the cowboy. However, he expects full supervisory control, so any time she attempts even the most minor ad-libbing, he expresses real disdain. Perhaps a parallel to Eastwood's own controlling instincts on his films directed by others, it is used merely as a minor character conflict here. As head of the show, Billy is essentially its director, trying to bring the old west into the modern world. Eastwood as a director of western films often brings a modern twist to the old west.

One of the most revealing aspects of the characters is their not being actual cowboys and Indians at all. They are draft dodgers, alcoholics, and ex-cons; even Billy is only a former shoe salesman who did time for shooting his wife after she slept with his best friend. This background information shows how Billy adheres to the code of the old west in his private life as well as his public performance, despite not having been raised in the old west. So his show is a phony, with fake cowboys and a threadbare existence. But the outcasts who have banded together to pull it off continue to believe in it.

Billy is attracted to, and supportive of, fellow outcasts, to the point where the troupe regularly performs free for patients in a mental institution. He recognizes the heiress as an outcast despite her being a woman of means. But the group's attempts to secure money in the old west style fails miserably (e.g., attempting to rob a train, realizing that modern transportation is not a slow moving locomotive).

Each film Eastwood directs exhibits how he utilizes his influences and continues to hone his own style. In *Bronco Billy*, he uses close-ups and quick reaction shots for comedy rather than drama, the shots being of double takes in reaction to the scene. His establishing shots, especially the opening scene, give us an understanding of the world he inhabits. Eastwood cuts from close-ups to medium shots, finally offering a long shot in which all of the contents within the frame offer a mise-en-scène that clearly presents the lack of attendance, and lack of success. Long shots are used during some of the performance segments, the performers surrounded by vast negative space within the contents of a tattered circus tent.

Janet Maslin's impressed review for the *New York Times* praised *Bronco Billy* perhaps beyond its worth:

> In a scene midway through *Bronco Billy*, the best and funniest Clint Eastwood movie in quite a while, the cowboy of the title strides into

a bank. And he starts to cash a check for $3, because in this movie all of the nice people are poor. Suddenly, two bank robbers burst in, and they scare a little boy, one of many innocent customers in the place. The little boy drops his piggy bank and it shatters. This is too much for Bronco Billy. He gives the bandits The Look, an indignant squint that means, roughly translated, "Grrr," and then he hauls off and fires away. What makes all this unusual for Mr. Eastwood, who directed the disarmingly boyish *Bronco Billy* and stars in the title role, is that the cowboy is more interested in the child than he is in the holdup men, and that he shoots the villains fairly politely, as if he didn't mean to do them any harm. Indeed, Mr. Eastwood is almost playing a very large Peter Pan. The locale may be Idaho instead of never-never land, but the feeling is that of a fairy tale, as Bronco Billy wanders through the West with a troupe of lost boys and girls. This is an emphatically American fable, which is perhaps why it ends with a chorus of "Stars and Stripes Forever." Miss Locke's role calls for a lot of brittle posturing at the outset, she adopts a broadly sardonic manner that makes the exaggeration seem funny. And Mr. Eastwood turns Billy, described as being "a big kid in a man's body" by the screenplay, into one of his warmest and most memorable characters.

Mr. Eastwood's direction constantly juxtaposes the old West and the new, as when Billy and the gang try to rob a modern train, and it whizzes right by them with utter indifference. Mr. Eastwood is still sticking to his guns, so to speak, the ideals of the contemporary western, newly fashionable right now, have been as prevalent in his last few films as they are this time. But *Bronco Billy* expresses these sentiments a shade more clearly, and moves along at a quicker, more consistent pace. Mr. Eastwood, who can be as formidable behind the camera as he is in front of it, is an entertainer, too.

The idea that *Bronco Billy* was a box office flop is incorrect. It made five times its production costs, delivering a $15 million profit to the studio. Eastwood, going through a divorce at the time, was protecting his assets, which is why this is the first movie since *Paint Your Wagon* (1969) that was not credited to his Malpaso Productions but is instead produced by the hastily and creatively assembled "second street productions." But while the film did make money, it did not meet expectations, and Eastwood considers it a box office disappointment. It also remains one of the films of which he is most proud.

In the biographical piece "Eastwood: In His Own Words" for the American Film Institute, Eastwood stated:

> None of the pictures I take a risk in cost a lot, so it doesn't take much for them to turn a profit. *Bronco Billy* cost five million. We sold it to TV for ten. We don't deal in big budgets. We know what we want

and we shoot it and we don't waste anything. I never understand these films that cost twenty, thirty million dollars when they could be made for half that. Maybe it's because no one cares. We care.

Perhaps it can be argued that a comedy like *Bronco Billy* was too far outside of Eastwood's niche. *Every Which Way but Loose* worked because the character he played was still a rough sort that fit his personality and appearance. Billy is a more idealistic and lighthearted character, and Eastwood is too gruff. This film benefits from Eastwood's directorial talents, but it might have worked better had someone else played the title role. Of course this is not to say that Eastwood the actor turns in a bad performance. He brings to the role an area of his talents that he had little opportunity to exhibit. But there is a basic gruffness that he adds to the role that sometimes clashes with the lighthearted framework of the character. Eastwood admitted himself in various interviews that he realizes he comes off better when playing winners rather than losers, especially since that is what his audience expects of him. But this was as much an idealistic effort for Eastwood the filmmaker as Bronco Billy's on-screen endeavors had been.

It was five years before Clint Eastwood returned to the western genre, and this time with the most conventional approach since *Joe Kidd*. Prior to that, he explored more ideas as an actor and filmmaker, continuing to explore opportunities that challenged his image, and making only one movie that was surefire box office. Unfortunately, the 1980s did not start out as aesthetically significant as the 1970s had been.

Note

1. Eastwood was in the middle of divorce proceedings, so a bogus production company other than Malpaso was created for this film's credits.

CHAPTER 17

Between the Westerns (1981–1985)

Cinema had changed pretty significantly since Eastwood broke into films in the 1950s, and he was one of the maverick filmmakers who moved us from the classic era. When Arthur Penn's *Bonnie and Clyde* was released in 1967, giving 1930s gangsters the counterculture attitudes of 1960s-era hippies, it ushered in a new perspective. Young filmmakers like Martin Scorsese, Francis Ford Coppola, Steven Spielberg, and George Lucas offered more personal projects, sometimes informed by nostalgia and sentiment, often exploring edgier ideas and different uses than the conventional cinematic forms. Eastwood became one of those maverick filmmakers, offering new and different ideas on some of cinema's most established genres, especially the western.

However, with the release of movies like Steven Spielberg's *Jaws* (1975) and George Lucas's *Star Wars* (1977), marketing strategies for movies changed. Saturating the market with advertising to ensure a successful opening weekend at the box office, soon films became more manufactured than created. The perspective changed drastically.

This had little effect on Clint Eastwood, who spent much of the 1980s experimenting with other ideas, his penchant for taking creative chances continuing throughout the decade. Perhaps because he was smart enough to form his own production company as early as the late 1960s from money he received with his initial stardom (and from investors who had a similar vision), he was among the first to create personal projects.

Eastwood was not without business savvy, however. Responding to what he considered lesser box office numbers for *Bronco Billy* (1980), it was decided that a sequel to the massive hit *Every Which Way but Loose* (1978) would be Clint Eastwood's next production. *Any Which Way You Can* (1980) gathers all of the principals from the first movie (a replacement orangutan was used), and some critics considered it funnier than the first effort. It was another major box office success. *Firefox* (1981), his follow-up film to *Any Which Way You Can*, responded, at least in part, to the new cinema that had emerged since the success of films like *Jaws* (1975) and *Star Wars* (1977). From a business standpoint, market saturation with advertising in an effort to secure a hefty box office on opening weekend became the norm for cinematic distribution in America. But special effects were also being used more frequently. Along with the *Star Wars* films, effects-driven movies like *Blade Runner* (1982) became quite popular.

In the midst of this, Clint Eastwood made a movie in which effects were utilized perhaps more than any of his other films. But *Firefox* also offered the type of character study that Eastwood's self-directed productions liked to explore. Working under a disguise, the Eastwood character (a Vietnam veteran) spends most of the film hiding behind another identity just as he had contained his characters' emotions in other self-directed films. His character is haunted by his experiences as a POW as he investigates Russia's claim that they have invented a jet fighter that can be controlled by mental telepathy, allowing them to emerge victorious in the Cold War. Eastwood's character, Mitch, speaks Russian, is an ace helicopter pilot, and is the best man to investigate this claim. Eastwood was drawn to the character's flaws and weaknesses, so he set out to direct and star in what Richard Schickel calls "one of the most curious entries in the Eastwood filmography, for it his only movie to rely heavily on special visual effects and the only one to deal directly with the Cold War. He is thoroughly absorbed in genre style, unable to assert his own." It was not well received. *People* magazine called it "Luke Skywalker trapped in Dirty Harry's soul."

Eastwood follows this up with *Honkytonk Man* (1982), only the second film (after *The Beguiled* [1971] in which the character he plays dies). He plays Red Stovall, a traveling country singer who is dying of tuberculosis. Set in the 1930s, the character has some similarities to country music icons like Jimmy Rodgers and Hank Williams, the latter especially, who, in 1953, self-destructed and died on the road. After years of drifting, Red gets the chance to perform at the Grand Ole Opry, an achievement he considers a worthy culmination to his otherwise small-time career. There is some consensus that if Eastwood had not been a success, his career might have taken the same trajectory as the character in *Honkytonk Man*. Clint Eastwood told Roger Ebert for the *Chicago Sun Times*:

> I knew *Honkytonk Man* was very risky, with me playing a dying drunk hillbilly singer, but I liked the book, and I knew a lot of people who had been self-destructive like that, and I wanted to make it. I've died in two pictures now, and neither one was successful. *Honkytonk Man* and *Beguiled*.

Eastwood in *Honkytonk Man.*

Hence, despite changes in cinema's marketing and production strategies, Eastwood continued to retain respect for the classic traditions and continued to work
as a maverick filmmaker who was not afraid to take chances and challenge his
screen persona.

Perhaps the most significant film Eastwood made during the early part of
the 1980s was *Sudden Impact* (1983), the only film in the Dirty Harry series that
he directed himself, and the best of the series other than the first. Eastwood drew
from elements in both *Magnum Force* (1973) and *The Enforcer* (1976), taking
the flaws from either of those movies and offering a different twist. Vigilantism
is again the focus; a woman (Sondra Locke), whose sister endured a brutal series
of rapes, sets out to kill her sister's attackers. The sister is now catatonic, being
cared for in an institution. The rapists are found dead, shot through the genitals
and then through the head. Harry Callahan takes the case.

The comical aspects of the character utilized in *The Enforcer* are used here,
and they offset the parallel story involving the woman who tracks down and
kills her sister's attackers. The Callahan scenes offer colorful action and sardonic
dialogue, including the iconic "make my day" scene[1] as Harry foils a robbery at a
favorite diner. The scenes with the woman are shot in darkness, with a film noir
quality. The film edits back and forth between the two corresponding narratives
until they finally meet at the film's conclusion.

In his review for the *Chicago Reader*, Dave Kehr calls attention to Eastwood's "minimalism" making him "a perfect performer for the comedy of understatement and underreaction." Kehr further stated:

> Only Buster Keaton could express himself with less facial mobility, and the spirit of Keaton does return, in surprising ways, to inform *Sudden Impact*. Like Keaton, he is a center of calm in a chaotic world, coping with every crisis that comes down the pike with perfect equanimity. Eastwood's calm like Keaton's is a powerful temptation to fate; disaster rains down upon him, as if the gods were sangfroid. The opening sections of *Sudden Impact* suggest the cyclone finale of *Steamboat Bill Jr.*: wherever Buster goes, buildings collapse or race about him; wherever Dirty Harry goes, someone is pulling a stickup or tossing Molotov cocktails in the back seat of his car. These incidents pile up to the point of absurdity and considerably beyond, but while they're very funny in a black way, they're also establishing something essential about the character. Eastwood's calm differs from Keaton's in that it isn't a natural attribute, but the product of fierce self-control—a willful suppression of emotional energy, chiefly anger, that still boils beneath the surface, pounding in the lightning-bolt vein that crosses Eastwood's left temple. For Harry, this suppression is synonymous with the law; he polices himself as strictly as he polices the streets, silencing every emotional insurrection.

Sondra Locke's character is unlike the vigilantes presented in *Magnum Force*. They were acting in a robotic manner, exhibiting no real character development or backstory other than taking the cleaning up of crime to an extreme even beyond Harry's own top-level defiance. The woman in *Sudden Impact* seems justified in her actions, despite their uncompromising brutality. Casting Sondra Locke, with her thin, waiflike appearance, shows another element of her acting ability. In each of the Eastwood films she appears, Locke plays a different variation of the femme fatale character. Eastwood told Roger Ebert:

> The stronger the participation of the female characters, the better the movie. They knew that in the old days, when women stars were equally as important as men. Hepburn, Davis, Colbert. They had great faces and great voices. By the 1950s, somehow all the female roles became sort of glorified gals in blue jeans at the next-door barbecue. They'd lost their strength. Now they get a few lines, a little sex scene. I respect women more than that.

Sudden Impact was the most financially successful sequel to *Dirty Harry*, even outgrossing the original at the box office. It is also perhaps the only good film in the series other than the first, as both *Magnum Force* and *The Enforcer* were rather heavily flawed, and the forthcoming *The Dead Pool* (1988) wasn't much better. Eastwood's direction, his use of wide-screen images supplanted by brief cutaways of close-ups during the action sequences, continued to be effective. But it is the way Eastwood concentrates on the characters in *Sudden Impact* that causes it to stand out.

Harry and the woman meet during the course of his pursuing her. She realizes who he is, sleeping with him to throw him off track. He does not realize who she is, and he is blinded by his attraction to what he perceives as a compatible mate. There is an element of pursuit to the romantic drama as well as the detective drama, as Kehr points out, and Eastwood cleverly realizes each can be told simultaneously. When Harry finds out who she is (sneaking out in the middle of the night while she sleeps and checking her license plate), he realizes he cannot yield to her. As Kehr also points out in his review, yielding to her would destroy his ethical faith in the law, and since his ethics are the basis of his personality, it would, in essence, destroy Harry. Retaining all of the violence, humor, and excitement of the original, *Sudden Impact* is a more in-depth character study with Eastwood's direction an added element to its aesthetic superiority as a film.

Often Eastwood's choices misfired despite good intentions. *City Heat* (1984) was a comical send-up of his screen character, playing opposite Burt Reynolds, a different kind of 1970s icon whose work in bucolic comedies ensured his box office stardom. Reynolds's entire career wavered between solid comedy-dramas like *The Longest Yard* (1974) and enormous flops like Peter Bogdanovich's wrongheaded musical *At Long Last Love* (1975). The actor settled into a niche of rural comedies that proved to be strong box office at first; however, soon the shallow country comedies that Reynolds appeared in would fall out of vogue. While *Smokey and the Bandit* (1976) and *Cannonball Run* (1981) were hits, films like *Stroker Ace* (1983) and *Cannonball Run II* (1984) were disappointing. Reynolds used to quip, "I haven't had a hit movie since Joan Collins was a virgin!" The idea of teaming Reynolds in a cheeky crime comedy with Clint Eastwood seemed like a fun idea, but the results were embarrassing. Critic Roger Ebert, who had been supportive of both actors' work, gave the film one-half of a star and wondered in his review, "[H]ow do travesties like this get made?" With a screenplay co-written by Blake Edwards and direction by Richard Benjamin, the concept seemed like it would net good box office, but its returns were marginal.

Eastwood's next film, *Tightrope* (1984), was an improvement. While direction is credited to screenwriter Richard Tuggle, it is Eastwood who took over direction of the film. Ironically, because of the "Clint Eastwood Rule,"[2] Clint Eastwood was unable to receive credit for directing. *Tightrope* was somewhat offbeat for Eastwood, even though he plays a New Orleans cop who teams up with a feminist to capture an elusive serial rapist. Dealing with issues like sadomasochism, it is one of the darkest films in which Eastwood appears. *Tightrope* enjoyed commercial and critical success.

In 1985, Clint Eastwood was ready to make another western. This time, however, the film he chose to make took a more conventional approach. Eastwood told Michael Munn for his book *Clint Eastwood: Hollywood's Loner*:

> Westerns. A period gone by, the pioneer, the loner operating by himself, without benefit of society. It usually has something to do with some sort of vengeance; he takes care of the vengeance himself, doesn't call the police. Like Robin Hood. It's the last masculine frontier. Romantic myth, I guess, though it's hard to think about anything romantic today. In a Western you can think, Jesus, there was a time when man was alone, on horseback, out there where man hasn't spoiled the land yet.

Eastwood also related to Roger Ebert for the *Chicago Sun Times*:

> I feel very close to the western. There are not too many American art forms that are original. Most are derived from European art forms. Other than the western and jazz or blues, that's all that's really original. *High Plains Drifter* and *Pale Rider* both have elements of the classic westerns in them, mythological characters who drift in and have an effect on the people.

However, while most of Clint Eastwood's western films challenged and redefined the genre, *Pale Rider* embraced its conventions. Using the more traditional approach, Eastwood does not eschew his cinematic technique, and he continues to draw upon elements from past work. But the story is told, the characters are developed, and the conclusion is presented in a manner that most critics noticed as similar to the George Stevens western *Shane* (1953).

Notes

1. Eastwood has stated that he recognized the line as powerful in context, but he never thought it would become his signature line thereafter.

2. See chapter 14, "*The Outlaw Josey Wales*," for a more thorough description of this law and its origin.

CHAPTER 18

Pale Rider (1985)

(Produced by the Malpaso Company for Warner Brothers)
Director: Clint Eastwood
Screenplay: Michael Butler, Dennis Shryack
Producer: Clint Eastwood
Executive Producer: Fritz Manes
Associate Producer: David Valdes
Music: Lennie Niehaus
Cinematography: Bruce Surtees
Editing: Joel Cox
Cast: Clint Eastwood (Preacher); Michael Moriarty (Hull Barret); Carrie
    Snodgress (Sarah Wheeler); Chris Penn (Josh LaHood); Richard Dysart
    (Coy LaHood); Sydney Penny (Megan Wheeler); Richard Kiel (Club);
    Doug McGrath (Spider Conway); John Russell (Stockburn); Charles
    Hallahan (McGill); Marvin J. McIntyre (Jagou); Fran Ryan (Ma Blanken-
    ship); Richard Hamilton (Jed Blankenship); Graham Paul (Ev Gossage);
    Chuck Lafont (Eddie Conway); Jeffrey Weissman (Teddy Conway); Al-
    len Keller (Tyson); Tom Oglesby (Elam); Herman Poppe (Ulrik Lindquist);
    Kathleen Wygle (Bess Gossage); Terrence Evans (Jake Henderson); Jim
    Hitson (Biggs); Loren Adkins (Bossy); Thomas H. Friedkin (Miner Tom);
    S. A. Griffin (Deputy Folke); Jack Radosta (Deputy Grissom); Robert
    Winley (Deputy Kobold); Billy Drago (Deputy Mather); Jeffrey Josephson
    (Deputy Sedge); John Dennis Johnston (Deputy Tucker); Lloyd Nelson
    (Bank Teller); Jay K. Fishburn (Telegrapher); George Orrison (Station-
    master Whitey); Milton Murrill (Porter); Mike Munsey (Dentist); Keith Dillin
    (Blacksmith); Buddy Van Horn (Stage Driver); Fritz Manes, Glenn Wright
    (Stage Riders); Michael Adams, Clay Lilley, Gene Hartline, R. L. Tolbert,
    Clifford Happy, Ross Loney, Larry Randles, Mike McGaughy, Jerry Gatlin
    (Horsemen).
Budget: $6,900,000
Gross: $41,400,000

Release Date: June 28, 1985
Running Time: 115 minutes
Sound Mix: Dolby
Color: Technicolor
Aspect Ratio: 2.35: 1
Availability: DVD and Blu-ray (Warner Home Video)

By 1985, Clint Eastwood had surpassed the level of movie star and was already reaching an iconic status. In a Roper poll among young Americans, he placed at the top among famous people they most admired. In the spring of the same year, he attended a White House ceremony where President Reagan awarded National Medals of Art. That fall, he attended Washington's official state reception for Prince Charles and Princess Diana, which included dancing with the princess at her request.

During the summer, his latest film, *Pale Rider* (1985), appeared in theaters nationwide. With *Pale Rider*, Clint Eastwood not only offered his most conventional western since *Joe Kidd* (1972), he also created a film that saved the western genre. In 1980, the same year Eastwood released *Bronco Billy*, the epic failure *Heaven's Gate* was released, and it destroyed any interest the studios had in making another western. *Heaven's Gate* was directed by Michael Cimino, who had helmed Eastwood in *Thunderbolt and Lightfoot* (1974). Cimino went wildly over budget on *Heaven's Gate*, demanding as many as fifty retakes on some scenes, delaying filming until a cloud with a shape he liked floated into the frame, and other indulgences. When he finally completed the film, he delivered a work print to the studio, United Artists, which ran over five hours. The studio refused to release a film of that length, so Cimino pared it down to three hours and forty minutes. When the film premiered in November 1980, Vincent Canby said it was like "a forced four hour tour of one's own living room." The film was cut down to two hours and twenty-nine minutes, and rereleased in April 1981. Roger Ebert said it was "the most scandalous cinematic waste I have ever seen, and remember I saw *Paint Your Wagon*." The film destroyed United Artists, which was sold to MGM. It also ruined the industry's trust in allowing directors to work with larger budgets to create personal projects.

Five years after this cinematic debacle, the western film was practically nonexistent. Since Eastwood produced films for his own company, he had little trouble convincing Warner Bros. to do a western. Eastwood pointed out his own success within the genre, and he stated that the popular *Star Wars* films were little more than westerns set in space. He also brought up the fact that his own *The Outlaw Josey Wales* (1976) was the last financially successful western made. In the book *Clint Eastwood: Interviews* the actor-filmmaker told Michael Henry

Poster for *Pale Rider*.

that westerns had become less interesting because the masters of that form—Anthony Mann, Raoul Walsh, John Ford, Howard Hawks—were no longer active. He stated he made *Pale Rider* "to analyze the classic Western. You can still talk about sweat and hard work, about the spirit, about love for the land and ecology. And I think you can say all these things in the Western, in the classic mythological form." The narrative features the rudiments of George Stevens's classic western *Shane* (1953).

Pale Rider is not given a specific time frame for its setting, but studies have determined it likely takes place in the 1880s due to comments within the narrative about outlawing hydraulic mining. Eastwood has the film open in a jarring, violent manner, which had become something of a staple of his westerns, including those he did not direct himself. The comparison we can make is with the self-directed western *The Outlaw Josey Wales* as the film opens on a tranquil setting where miners and their families have settled in an area and are panning for gold. The tranquility of the setting is suddenly and jarringly interrupted by a group of marauders riding in, shooting, destroying the camp, and even killing a young girl's dog. The girl buries the dog and prays for a miracle just as a stranger comes riding into town. She believes him to be the answer to her prayer.

The setup has immediate similarities to *High Plains Drifter* (1973) upon the Eastwood character's entrance. In that film, he enters a very quiet town. In *Pale Rider*, he arrives as the town has quieted from a most recent attack. Among the first things the stranger does in *High Plains Drifter* is respond with stoicism to men confronting him in a saloon, later shooting them down when they physically accost him in a barber shop soon afterward. In *Pale Rider*, the stranger comes to the rescue of a man being attacked by a group of others, effectively beating them down. There is an element to every Eastwood western where the central figure he plays is able to thwart many attackers singlehandedly. This is another example. The man he rescues, Hull Barret (Michael Moriarty), the leader of the miners, invites the stranger to his house for dinner. He appears wearing a clerical collar and is thereafter referred to as Preacher. These initial scenes establish the character's abilities as well as a mystery about his backstory.

Eastwood liked having his character confronted by a group of people, and in those rare situations where it is a single person, it is a much larger man, or one who matches Eastwood in size. This is not always an easy dynamic to arrange as it would be for a more diminutive movie tough guy like James Cagney. Eastwood is over six feet tall. However, in *Pale Rider* the dynamic offered is opposite the massive, imposing Richard Kiel[1] who, as Club, towers over Preacher. Displaying just how mighty he is, the giant Club picks up a sledgehammer with one hand and smashes apart a large rock. When he confronts Preacher, however, he is hit with a sledgehammer in the face and groin. He staggers away in pain, the Preacher once again victorious in a situation that appeared to be especially challenging. It also shows how Eastwood has some interest in the dynamic between large and small, harking back to his kinship with midget actor Billy Curtis in *High Plains Drifter*. *Pale Rider* adds another, similar dynamic via Preacher's relationship with the worshipful little girl who had prayed for what he symbolically represents.

The similarities to *Shane* become clearer not only in regard to Preacher and Megan, but also the narrative that deals with a group of miners who unite against crooked people attempting to take control. Preacher is the same sort of mysterious stranger that Shane was; both are experienced with gunslinging, and both attempt to help the laborers. Alan Ladd, who played the title role in *Shane*, was a small, slightly built man, but he made a career playing hard-boiled detectives and other commanding roles. While his character is not unlike the sort of persona Eastwood had established, he did not have Clint's size or presence. Shane is experienced with guns but offers little experience with his fists. When he is confronted, it is his shooting ability that controls his environment. Preacher can also fight, and win, against as many as a half-dozen men.

There are a lot of complexities to the Preacher character. The screenplay had been developed by Michael Butler and Dennis Shryack, who had written

The Gauntlet, and they offered Eastwood a role that had layers tucked beneath the stoicism he outwardly exhibited. There is religious allegory, environmental prophecy, and literary symbolism abounding in the actions and manner of the character. As Eastwood would later tell interviewer Christopher Frayling:

> *Pale Rider* is kind of allegorical, more in the *High Plains Drifter* mode: like that, though he isn't a reincarnation or anything, but he does ride a pale horse like the four horsemen of the apocalypse. . . . It's a classic story of the big guys against the little guys . . . the corporate mining which ends up in hydraulic mining, they just literally mow the mountains away, you know, the trees and everything . . . all that was outlawed in California some years ago, and they still do it in Montana and a few places.

There are distractions and temptations (a widow, played by Carrie Snodgress; the worshipful child; money that is offered to the miners by corporate interests; etc.). And, as with the conclusion of *Shane*, Preacher rides off at the end of the movie with the voice of a loving youngster calling behind him, echoing on the soundtrack as the movie ends.

The movie's title is biblically inspired:

> And I looked, and behold a pale horse: and his name that sat on him was Death, and Hell followed with him. (Revelation 6:8)

The Preacher arrives in answer to a prayer. He seems to have a mysterious, mystical quality, able to evade people in a gunfight by seeming to disappear. He comes from nowhere; he leaves when the job is done. This is also the character element in *Shane* but which does not include the same religious allegory.

Editorial writer Stephen Chapman discussed the religious angle in his story "Who Is the Pale Rider?" for the *Chicago Tribune*:

> The Preacher's efficiency at bloodshed, though always in self-defense, is hard to reconcile with our image of the Savior. Eastwood has portrayed a different Jesus: the one who brought not peace but a sword, the one of Revelation who raises the righteous into heaven and casts the wicked into the depths. His is an unusual reinterpretation. Still, it is these pervasive Christian elements that give the film its peculiar resonance. Eastwood has tried to breathe new life not only into the western, but into the greatest story ever told.

It is not only *Shane* or the Bible that appear to have inspired *Pale Rider*. Eastwood's interest in doing a more traditionally structured western also resulted in the resurrection of the genre's most noted clichés—ones that the western film tried to avoid as too archaic and corny for the modern era, including as far back as the 1953 film. *Pale Rider* offers a silent showdown on the town's main street. There is a scene where a group of cowboys shoot at another's feet, instructing him to dance. And it is a film with the very clichés that were at one time said to have helped make the western less interesting for younger generations that helped save the genre from extinction as the result of an indulgent box office flop.

Eastwood proved his point with *Pale Rider*, that his track record with the western would net a hit, even after *Heaven's Gate* had obliterated any interest in revisiting the genre. *Pale Rider* was made for a budget of under $7 million and grossed over $40 million at the box office. It was also entered into the 1985 Cannes Film Festival.

Along with Moriarty and Snodgress, actor Richard Dysart's notable portrayal of Sydney Penny, the land baron who wants to get rid of the miners and explore the land's riches for himself, is worth mention. Eastwood liked to surround himself with top-level performers who responded well to his efficient method of working.

With *Pale Rider*, Eastwood's continued growth as a filmmaker was becoming more evident, while his box office power was so enormous it allowed him to make a film in a genre considered obsolete and singlehandedly make it once again feasible for Hollywood to produce westerns. By the end of the decade, *Young Guns* (1988), with its youthful cast that included twenty-something actors Kiefer Sutherland and Charlie Sheen, made the genre palatable for even younger moviegoers. The following year, the western TV miniseries *Lonesome Dove* was one of the highest and most acclaimed programs of its time.

Roger Ebert stated in his review for the *Chicago Sun Times*:

> Clint Eastwood has by now become an actor whose moods and silences are so well known that the slightest suggestion will do to convey an emotion. No actor is more aware of his own instruments, and Eastwood demonstrates that in *Pale Rider*, a film he dominates so completely that only later do we realize how little we really saw of him. Instead of filling each scene with his own image and dialogue, Eastwood uses sleight of hand: We are shown his eyes, or a corner of his mouth, or his face in shadow, or his figure with strong light behind it. He has few words. The other characters in the movie project their emotions upon him. He may indeed be the pale rider suggested in the title, whose name was death, but he may also be an avenging spirit, come back from the grave to confront the man who murdered him. One of the subtlest things in the movie is the way it plays with the possibility that Eastwood's character may be a ghost, or at least something other than an ordinary mortal. Other things in the movie are not so subtle. In its broad outlines, *Pale Rider* is a traditional

Western, with a story that has been told, in one form or another, a thousand times before. But "Pale Rider" is, over all, a considerable achievement, a classic Western of style and excitement. Many of the greatest Westerns grew out of a director's profound understanding of the screen presence of his actors; consider, for example, John Ford's films with John Wayne and Henry Fonda. In *Pale Rider*, Clint Eastwood is the director, and having directed himself in nine previous films, he understands so well how he works on the screen that the movie has a resonance that probably was not even there in the screenplay.

After the release of *Pale Rider*, Eastwood directed a film for TV, *Vanessa in the Garden* (1985), from a script by Steven Spielberg. Sondra Locke was one of the cast members. It would be another seven years before Clint Eastwood would produce another western, but *Unforgiven* (1992) would be a perfect culmination of his films in this genre. Meanwhile, the actor and director used his star power to continue exploring other possibilities. But as Clint Eastwood closed out the 1980s, some of his films responded to the period of cinematic consumption over inquiry, while others were deeply personal projects that netted limited box office. In any case, Eastwood continued to investigate a variety of different ideas with uneven results.

Note

1. In a few years, Kiel would become infamous as the gold-toothed James Bond villain Jaws in *The Spy Who Loved Me* (1977).

CHAPTER 19

Between the Westerns (1986–1991)

As the 1980s became the 1990s, Clint Eastwood extended his range beyond show business by entering the political arena. He served as mayor of Carmel, California, from 1986 to 1988. During that time, he made only two movies, *Heartbreak Ridge* (1986) and the final Dirty Harry film *The Dead Pool* (1988). Eastwood directed *Heartbreak Ridge*, a rough drama about Tom Highway (Eastwood), an old-school marine type whose methods conflict with the young recruits whose attitudes come from a more modern, and decidedly lazier, era. Eastwood told Roger Ebert at the time:

> Maybe I'm just sort of a contrarian. It just seemed like the most interesting thing about this story was the personal relationships. This is a guy who has been in the military since he was very young, and all of a sudden he's facing retirement, and that's it, and where does he go? I've made those Rambo-style pictures where one guy goes out and wins the war, and they're fun, but they don't have much to say. The thing about the Ramboesque pictures is, you got to figure if there were 10 guys like that, how'd we lose the war in the first place? Another thing. As a director, I'm more interested in the whole story—in other people's characters. If I were only acting, maybe I'd want to be the only guy in the movie. Who can say?

After being off screen throughout 1987, Clint Eastwood made one more Dirty Harry movie. *The Dead Pool* was directed by Clint Eastwood's longtime stuntman Buddy Van Horn, although it is likely Eastwood offered some contribution behind the camera. Notable today as being an early screen appearance by Jim Carrey, *The Dead Pool* is the weakest of the Harry pictures, prone to easy situations, convenient effects, and a general lack of commitment from all involved. It is superficially entertaining in that the character is such an icon, any

153

appearance is appreciated, but *The Dead Pool* is even less effective than *Magnum Force* (1973) or *The Enforcer* (1976) had been. Surprisingly, critics Roger Ebert and Gene Siskel, who had become popular in the mainstream with a TV show discussing the latest movies, each called it the best Dirty Harry film since the original. However, even though it grossed nearly $40 million at the box office, it was the least profitable of the five Harry Callahan films. In a 2000 interview with Marc Eliot, Eastwood indicated he would make no more Dirty Harry movies, joking about the possibilities of further sequels:

> *Dirty Harry VI!* Harry is retired. He's standing in a stream, fly-fishing. He gets tired of using the pole—and BA-BOOM! Or Harry is retired, and he catches bad guys with his walker.

Because of his interest in jazz, Eastwood served as executive producer on the documentary *Thelonius Monk: Straight No Chaser* (1988), which led to a more personal project, *Bird* (1988), featuring Forest Whitaker as the brilliant but tragic saxophone great Charlie "Bird" Parker. Eastwood produced and directed this labor of love, resulting in another aspect of his ability being taken quite seriously. There was still belief in some quarters that Eastwood was merely an action star whose direction was derivative and without much personal vision. Such a

Eastwood played Harry Callahan for the final time in *The Dead Pool.*

perspective had already been proven wrong, but the shortsightedness of such critics was obliterated entirely with his sensitive, insightful look at the jazz great.

After the simplistic throwaway comedy *Pink Cadillac* (1989), Eastwood produced and directed another personal project called *White Hunter, Black Heart* (1990). Starring as a director named John Wilson (based on John Huston), the film chronicles the director's obsession with hunting elephants, despite his personal misgivings, while shooting a movie on location in Africa (which, in Huston's case, would have been the 1951 classic *The African Queen*). While some critical appreciation was received, *White Hunter, Black Heart* lost money at the box office.

Eastwood came back with a cop-buddy movie, *The Rookie* (1990), which he also directed, from a script by Boaz Yakin and Scott Spiegel. According to Spiegel, in an interview with the author, any issues that other writers might have had with Eastwood's controlling approach to their work were absent on this film:

> Clint was awesome, one of the all time great people to work with. I was inspired to use the climax to *Play Misty for Me* for Charlie Sheen's motorcycle chase to save Lara Flynn Boyle in *The Rookie*. I told Clint that and he said, "It worked then, it'll work now." *The Rookie* was shot mostly nights, and at one point it was 4 a.m. at San Jose International Airport. Clint, a bit tired from directing and starring in the film, sat down next to me and said, "Next time write a movie that takes place during the day." Clint would sit at lunch with us and feed us lobster, lamb chops—he really took care of his crew.

Critics were generally unimpressed with *The Rookie*, believing it to be a by-the-numbers action movie too similar to what Eastwood had done before. It earned over $20 million at the box office and has held up as an exciting film with a strong cast. That it was a pleasurable experience for those involved might have something to do with its continued appeal.

After *The Rookie*, Eastwood was off screen for all of 1991; he then returned the following year with his final western. *Unforgiven* (1992) turned out to be the perfect culmination of his films in this genre as well as one of the finest American western films in motion picture history.

CHAPTER 20

Unforgiven (1992)

(A Warner Bros.–Malpaso Production)
Director: Clint Eastwood
Screenplay: David Webb Peoples
Producer: Clint Eastwood
Associate Producer: Julian Ludwig
Executive Producer: David Valdes
Music: Lennie Niehaus
Cinematography: Jack N. Green
Editing: Joel Cox
Cast: Clint Eastwood (Bill Munny); Gene Hackman (Little Bill Daggett); Morgan Freeman (Ned Logan); Richard Harris (English Bob); Jaimz Woolvett (The Schofield Kid); Saul Rubinek (W. W. Beauchamp); Frances Fisher (Strawberry Alice); Anna Thomson (Delilah Fitzgerald); David Mucci (Quick Mike); Rob Campbell (Davey Boy Bunting); Anthony James (Skinny Dubois); Tara Dawn Fredrick (Little Sue); Beverley Elliott (Silky); Liisa Repo-Martell (Faith); Josie Smith (Crow Creek Kate); Shane Meier (Will Munny); Aline Levasseur (Penny Munny); Cherrilene Cardinal (Sally Two Trees); Robert Koons (Crocker); Ron White (Clyde Ledbetter); Mina E. Mina (Muddy Chandler); Henry Kope (German Joe Schultz); Jeremy Ratchford (Deputy Andy Russell); John Pyper-Ferguson (Charley Hecker); Jefferson Mappin (Fatty Rossiter); Walter Marsh (Barber); Garner Butler (Eggs Anderson); Larry Reese (Tom Luckinbill); Blair Haynes (Paddy McGee); Frank C. Turner (Fuzzy); Sam Karas (Thirsty Thurston); Lochlyn Munro (Texas Slim); Ben Cardinal (Johnny Foley); Philip Hayes (Lippy MacGregor); Michael Charrois (Wiggens); Bill Davidson (Buck Barthol); Larry Joshua (Bucky); George Orrison (The Shadow); Gregory Goossen (Fighter); Paul McLean, James Herman, Michael Maurer (People on the Train).
Working Titles: *The Cut Whore Killings; The William Munny Killings*
Budget: $14,400,000 (estimated)
Gross: $101,157,447 (USA)

Release Date: August 7, 1992
Running Time: 131 minutes
Sound Mix: Dolby Stereo
Color: Technicolor
Aspect Ratio: 2.35: 1
Availability: DVD and Blu-ray (Warner Home Video)

Unforgiven was released nearly thirty years after the initial Italian release of *A Fist-ful of Dollars*, and when examining Clint Eastwood's western films, it serves as the perfect culmination. Directing as well as starring, Eastwood utilizes virtually all of the elements he learned throughout the evolutionary process of his western movies, exhibiting how he had consistently honed them over the decades.

Eastwood was alerted to David Webb Peoples's screenplay as early as 1976 and had already planned to develop it. He chose to wait because he wanted to be old enough to play the central character, and also realized it would be a fitting conclusion to his western films. While maintaining this property, Eastwood would make both *The Outlaw Josey Wales* (1976) and *Pale Rider* (1985) as well as several films outside of the western genre, finally deciding after reaching age sixty that his screen persona was weathered enough to tackle this project. It was shot between August and November 1991. Peoples, meanwhile, had since scored with the screenplays for *Blade Runner* (1982) and *Ladyhawke* (1985), among others.

As with many of his most effective westerns, Eastwood opens *Unforgiven* by showing a despicable violent act when two cowboys slice up a young prostitute's face, disfiguring her for life, destroying her beauty and, ultimately, her liveli-hood. When the town's sheriff, Little Bill Daggett (Gene Hackman), is lenient with the cowboys and lets them go free, the brothel puts up a $1,000 bounty[1] for the killing of Quick Mike and Davey Boy (David Mucci, Rob Campbell).

This incident is set in Wyoming, and alerts an ambitious young cowboy who calls himself The Schofield Kid (Jaimz Wolvett). He visits the pig farm of William Munny (Eastwood) to recruit his services in killing the cowboys and sharing the bounty. By all accounts, Munny is a hardworking farmer, widowed with two small children, and has no interest in this pursuit. However, through the dialogue, it is revealed that the now repentant Munny was at one time the meanest bandit in the west, even to the point of killing women and children without remorse. An older man who has mellowed and removed himself com-pletely from this past life, Munny initially refuses. However, his limited success with farming, his single-parent status, and the uncertain financial future of his children causes him to change his mind.

Unlike *The Outlaw Josey Wales*, Eastwood's protagonist is not an innocent farmer who is thrust into violence due to a heinous act perpetrated on his loved ones; he is a former killer who has built a wall around himself with a new life and a family. While in both films his character is doing what he feels is necessary for his family, the approaches are very different (vengeance in one, financial necessity in the other). The stoicism of Josey Wales stemmed from the hurt that evolved into bitterness. In *Unforgiven* it is a man attempting to emotionally overpower his past deeds with a new life. His calm is such a strong element of his character, and the dialogue continually reminds us what a despicable killer this man once was. And since this time his killing will be one of vengeance against someone who committed an act as hideous as he might have once done himself, it also represents the ultimate repentance. Munny is, in effect, setting out to symbolically destroy what he once was.

The unlikely partnership element that Eastwood's westerns often revisit is already presented in *Unforgiven* via the stoic veteran gunfighter Munny alongside the boastful, hotheaded Kid. This relationship is anchored when Munny insists on including his old partner Ned Logan (Morgan Freeman). Logan is the firm, calming presence who understands Munny and keeps the ambitious Kid at bay. The character dynamics here blend neatly to not only maintain the narrative, but also give different perspectives to the pursuit. Ned Logan does not have the youthful ambition of the Kid or the financial need of Munny. His agreeing to engage in the pursuit is borne out of loyalty to his old partner. Also settled with a wife and far from his gunfighter past, Ned believes he owes Munny his presence.

Eastwood in *Unforgiven*.

It is still early in the film when the story explores the limitations a much older William Munny must confront as he attempts to engage in what he had effectively done as a much younger man. Years of tranquil family life on a farm that is secluded from other people and activities, perhaps decades past such a pursuit as this, Munny's response to riding in a rainstorm is a fever, but he stubbornly refuses to slow down and acknowledge lack of strength and immunity. When they finally arrive in Wyoming at the brothel, Munny sits quietly in a saloon, attempting to recover. Sheriff Daggett allows no violence in his territory; realizing why Munny is there but not who he is, Daggett, along with some deputies, confronts the stranger. Munny is beaten and thrown out of the saloon. He is nursed back to health by Ned and the Kid.

The Munny character exhibits the same personality traits as the usual Eastwood western protagonist as far back as the Sergio Leone westerns. There is a certain level of character growth throughout his western films, going from the lone young gunfighter to playing ethereal characters and family men. In *Unforgiven*, Eastwood's screen persona is a despicable man who has become human in his old age. He does not kill children; he has kids of his own. He does not tough out the elements; instead, he gets sick. The sickness results in a weakened condition, and he becomes the victim of a strict lawman.

The concept of law and order is also skewed. Now that Munny has set out to kill a killer, to destroy the guilty rather than the innocent, he is thwarted by the lawman who let the cowboys go free. The sheriff, therefore, comes off as the bad guy in this situation. Munny is out for the same vengeance that the viewer would expect the young cowboys deserve. The loyal and understanding Ned Logan appears to be the most sympathetic character at this point, causing us to forget that he had once also been a lawbreaking gunfighter. After spending his western film career defying the genre's conventions, Eastwood gives us a film in which even the underlying structure of his own defiant past productions is challenged. There are no good guys here, just bad guys who have chosen to do a good thing—but this good thing is murder, however emotionally justified it may be. Also, their intention is not due to compassion, but for the money. Munny's remorse at some areas of his gunslinging past is evident in this dialogue:

> Munny: Ned, you remember that drover I shot through the mouth and his teeth came out the back of his head? I think about him now and again. He didn't do anything to deserve to get shot, at least nothin' I could remember when I sobered up.
>
> Ned: You ain't like that no more.
>
> Munny: That's right. I'm just a fella now. I ain't no different than anyone else no more.

The attempt at returning to their past becomes especially daunting for Ned and Munny once the latter is nursed back to health and they find one of the cowboys they are pursuing. After ambushing a group of cowboys and killing Davey Boy, both Ned and Munny feel a level of remorse they had never encountered in their younger days. It is too much for Ned, who has no stake in the process other than loyalty to his partner. He leaves the group to return home, Munny insisting he still get a third of the reward once the job is completed. Munny and the Kid venture on after Ned has left. They arrive at a ranch where the Kid discovers Quick Mike in an outhouse and shoots him dead. He and Munny escape the wrath of the other cowboys. The Kid confesses to Munny that he had never killed another man before, and despite the justification of killing someone who had hurt another, he is distraught and renounces the life of a gunfighter. "I ain't like you," he tells Munny. Munny is also no longer like his former self.

There is a fascinating element to the perspective of the central figures in *Unforgiven*. While Eastwood's westerns defied convention from the Leone-directed Dollars trilogy onward, their defiance stemmed from a greater level of violence and unbridled pummeling of the western movie's code and conventions. *Unforgiven* responds to that defiance and to the violence. William Munny had been worse than any of the past characters Eastwood might have played. The way his past is described, Munny might have been closer to the notorious Scorpio in *Dirty Harry* (1971), but without the jittery cowardice of that character. Every gunslinger in *Unforgiven* is remorseful and repentant, right down to the boastful Kid, who had claimed to have killed five men. It was a lie, he is a phony, and the one killing he does accomplish causes him to be consumed with guilt. He vows to never kill again. Munny understands.

However, Munny's own perspective changes when one of the younger prostitutes from the brothel meets up with him and the Kid to give them their reward. She reveals that Ned was captured by Daggett on his way back home and beaten to death. She further states that Ned's corpse is on display in a coffin in front of a saloon. The Kid is instructed to deliver the money to Ned's wife and Munny's children. Munny sets out to avenge the murder of his partner. Now that the violence for which he seeks vengeance is against one of his own, Munny has no trouble returning to his past persona. The man who admits to having killed "anything that ran, walked, or crawled," now has a personal purpose in once again embracing such an attitude.

Daggett is in the process of gathering a posse to go after Munny and the Kid when Munny enters and points a rifle at the men who are gathered. He coldly pulls the trigger and blows away the saloon proprietor, causing Daggett to react incredulously.

> Daggett: I can't believe it! You just killed an unarmed man!
>
> Munny: Well, he should have armed himself.

Munny plans to blow away Daggett, despite the lawman's stating that as soon as the trigger is pulled, the men surrounding him will kill Munny. However, the gun misfires, so Daggett quickly orders his men to shoot Munny dead. Munny throws his rifle at Daggett, pulls out a pistol, and effectively blows away several of the men, including Daggett. Those who remain standing are told to leave. Daggett has not yet died, and Munny stands over him. "I'll see you in hell," the lawman says to the gunfighter. Munny then shoots him dead.

At this point it is necessary to discuss a tangential subplot in which a city-bred writer named Beauchamp (Saul Rubinek), traveling west looking for ideas for his next novel, has found his way to this very saloon during the course of the narrative, and witnesses the gunfight between Munny, Daggett, and Daggett's assembled posse. Earlier in the film, the writer had hooked up with English Bob (Richard Harris)[2] who was offering some tall tales in order to be the subject for Beauchamp's next literary work. When he is humiliated and run out of town by Daggett, he is revealed as far beneath the stories he'd been offering the writer. Some critics, including both Gene Siskel and Roger Ebert, argued that English Bob was an unnecessary element in the film, never even meeting up with the narrative's main characters. However, this tangential plot provides character elements of Daggett, who figures significantly, and Beauchamp's presence at the end of the film allows clarity in the movie's conclusion. Searching for ideas, never finding much to explore, Beauchamp actually gets to witness a gunfight, obviously the final one, from a noted gunfighter. Munny's legacy will be recorded for posterity as it concludes. He returns to his children, the reward money allowing them all to relocate where Munny plies another trade that is more lucrative.

Unforgiven is shown in the closing credits to be dedicated "To Sergio and Don," Eastwood's strongest filmmaking mentors. Both Leone and Siegel had died by this time (Siegel only a few months before production began). Eastwood's direction is superb, using all that he'd learned from these men as well as his own decades of experience. His long shots framing the action with beautiful scenery in the negative space is assisted by veteran production designer Henry Bumstead, whose skills enhance each shot. It took Bumstead a remarkably short thirty-two days to construct the Big Whiskey set, the fastest in his career. Eastwood's notorious efficiency resulted in the film being completed four days ahead of schedule. It became the first Clint Eastwood film to win an Oscar for Best Picture, and only the third western to do so (the others being *Cimarron* in 1931 and *Dances with Wolves* in 1990). Eastwood also won for Best Director, Joel Cox for Best Film Editing, and Gene Hackman for Best Supporting Actor.

Gene Hackman had received the script back in the 1970s and turned it down before it found its way to Eastwood. When Eastwood finally decided to film it, he wanted Hackman for the Daggett role. Hackman was concerned that it might glorify gun violence. Eastwood, also a gun control supporter, assured him that it did not. Once completed, it can be argued that *Unforgiven* has an antiviolence message lurking beneath the surface of its narrative.

Vincent Canby of the *New York Times* was pleased with the film, but felt its scope was beyond director Eastwood's grasp:

> Time has been good to Clint Eastwood. If possible, he looks even taller, leaner and more mysteriously possessed than he did in Sergio Leone's seminal *Fistful of Dollars* a quarter of a century ago. The years haven't softened him. They have given him the presence of some fierce force of nature, which may be why the landscapes of the mythic, late 19th-century West become him, never more so than in his new *Unforgiven*. As written by David Webb Peoples and directed by Mr. Eastwood, *Unforgiven* is a most entertaining western that pays homage to the great tradition of movie westerns while surreptitiously expressing a certain amount of skepticism. Mr. Eastwood has learned a lot from his mentors, including the great Don Siegel (*Two Mules for Sister Sara* and *The Beguiled*, among others), a director with no patience for sentimentality. *Unforgiven*, which has no relation to *The Unforgiven*, the 1960 John Huston western, never quite fulfills the expectations it so carefully sets up. It doesn't exactly deny them, but the bloody confrontations that end the film appear to be purposely muted, more effective theoretically than dramatically. This, I suspect, is a calculated risk. Mr. Eastwood doesn't play it safe as a director, but there are times in *Unforgiven*, as in his jazz epic, *Bird*, that the sheer scope of the narrative seems to overwhelm him. It's not easy cramming so much information into a comparatively limited amount of time. Toward the end of *Bird*, he didn't seem to be telling the story of Charlie Parker as much as letting it unravel. That doesn't happen in *Unforgiven*, but the tone, so self-assured to begin with, becomes loaded with qualifications. The film looks great, full of broad chilly landscapes and skies that are sometimes as heavy with portents as those in something by El Greco. It's corny but it works.

Roger Ebert was rather unimpressed with the film upon its initial 1992 release, but later changed his mind. First offering only a two-and-a-half-star rating, Ebert later proclaimed the film to be a four-star masterpiece. In a 2002 essay on his Great Movies website, Roger Ebert stated:

> Clint Eastwood's *Unforgiven* takes place at that moment when the old West was becoming new. Professional gunfighters have become such an endangered species that journalists follow them for stories. Men who slept under the stars are now building themselves houses. William Munny, "a known thief and a murderer," supports himself

with hog farming. The violent West of legend lives on in the memories of men who are by 1880 joining the middle class. Within a few decades, Wyatt Earp would be hanging around Hollywood studios, offering advice. Eastwood chose this period for *Unforgiven*, I suspect, because it mirrored his own stage in life. He began as a young gunslinger on TV and in the early Sergio Leone films *A Fistful of Dollars* and *For a Few Dollars More*, and he matured in *Coogan's Bluff* and *Two Mules for Sister Sara*, under the guidance of Don Siegel, the director he often cited as his mentor. Now Eastwood was in his 60s, and had long been a director himself. Leone had died in 1989 and Siegel in 1991; he dedicated *Unforgiven* to them. If the Western was not dead, it was dying; audiences preferred science fiction and special effects. It was time for an elegy.

The film reflects a passing era even in its visual style. The opening shot is of a house, a tree, and a man at a graveside. The sun is setting, on this man and the era he represents. Many of the film's exteriors are widescreen compositions showing the vastness of the land. The daytime interiors, on the other hand, are always strongly backlit, the bright sun pouring in through windows so that the figures inside are dark and sometimes hard to see. Living indoors in a civilized style has made these people distinct. If Clint Eastwood had not been a star, he would still figure as a major director, with important work in the Western, action and comedy genres, and unique films like *Bird* (1988), his biography of the saxophonist Charlie Parker, the love story *The Bridges of Madison County* (1995), and the wonderful *A Perfect World* (1993). . . . *Unforgiven*, too, uses a genre as a way to study human nature.

Unforgiven debuted at number 1 in its opening weekend, earning $15,018,007, making it the best opening for an Eastwood film up to that time. It remained at number 1 for three weeks. In its thirty-fifth week in release, it was still at number 8. When it finally closed on July 15, 1993, it had spent nearly a full year in theaters (343 days). Along with earning $101,157,447 in North America, it received another $58,000,000 overseas.

Critical praise was pretty much unanimous, and the recognition has continued. It was admitted to the National Film Registry in 2004 as an essential film of significant historical and aesthetic value. In 2008, the American Film Institute named it the fourth greatest western in the history of cinema, after *The Searchers* (1956), *High Noon* (1952), and *Shane* (1953).

Interestingly enough, a remake of *Unforgiven* was made in Japan in 2013, directed by Lee Sang-il and starring Ken Watanabe. The central character was a samurai, and the film took place during Japan's Melji period. Just as Eastwood's first major western was inspired by a Japanese samurai film, his final one came full circle and was remade in such a way in Japan.

Notes

1. Conservatively, this would be equivalent to roughly $125,000 now.
2. Harris would later claim that he was watching *High Plains Drifter* (1973) on television when Eastwood phoned him to offer the role of English Bob.

CHAPTER 21

After the Westerns

Clint Eastwood's career received a real boost after the success of *Unforgiven* (1992). Some state it saved the western; others believed it saved his career. Neither is completely accurate. *Pale Rider* (1985) had saved the western effectively a few years earlier, and while *The Dead Pool* (1988) is probably the only real box office success Eastwood enjoyed between the two westerns, this slump did not indicate a possible loss of his career. However, after *Unforgiven*, his clout was stronger than ever. Once again. Eastwood investigated other ideas, never one to settle too firmly into a niche. But these journeys became more infrequent, with Eastwood usually settling into familiar territory.

In 1993 Clint Eastwood appeared in Wolfgang Peterson's *In the Line of Fire* and his own *A Perfect World*, both films enjoying box office success. For the latter film, about a kidnapped boy who becomes friends with his captor (Kevin Costner), Eastwood, as the pursuing lawman, has roughly forty-five minutes of total screen time in the 138-minute film. He receives second billing (after Costner) for the first time since *Two Mules for Sister Sara* (1970) twenty-three years earlier.

Off screen in 1994, he returned the following year with the film version of the popular Robert James Waller novel *The Bridges of Madison County*. Most of Eastwood's films during the remainder of the 1990s and into the 2000s were pretty standard action movies, comfortable and familiar territory, but with uneven results. Films like *Absolute Power* (1997), *True Crime* (1999), and *Blood Work* (2002) were entertaining action dramas but unremarkable. *Space Cowboys* (2000) was the only departure from what had become something of a formula, about a group of retired astronauts in their seventies going into space to investigate a Russian satellite that has veered off course.

It was *Million Dollar Baby* (2004) that emerged as his best cinematic achievement since *Unforgiven*, winning Oscars for Best Picture, Best Actress

(Hilary Swank), Best Supporting Actor (Morgan Freeman), and Best Directing (Eastwood). At seventy-four, Eastwood became the oldest director to win an Oscar. At the Academy Award ceremonies, Eastwood's ninety-five-year-old mother was in attendance. The success of *Million Dollar Baby* allowed Clint Eastwood to pursue more personal cinematic projects such as *Flags of Our Fathers* (2006), about the six men who raised the flag at the Battle of Iwo Jima during World War II, and *Letters from Iwo Jima* (2006), which told of that battle from the perspective of the Japanese.

If *Unforgiven* is the culmination of Clint Eastwood's western film legacy, *Gran Torino* (2008) might be considered the culmination of Dirty Harry. Eastwood does not specifically play Harry Callahan in *Gran Torino*, but the character contains all of the same elements as if it were showing a retired Harry in old age. His character of Walt Kowalsky offers the same cantankerous defiance and knee-jerk prejudices as Harry had exhibited, each with more muttering sarcasm as the character aged. Even while the film was in production, rumors spread that it would be a final culminating installment in the Dirty Harry franchise. There is only one death in the entire film, and it is Clint's character, who dies violently. *Gran Torino* became, in box office terms, Eastwood's biggest moneymaker.[1]

Eastwood's iconic status continued into the twenty-first century. As he aged, he continued to play aging characters who were stubborn and unsettled about getting older, such as in Robert Lorenz's *Trouble with the Curve* (2012). As a

Eastwood in *Gran Torino.*

director, he continued to investigate new genres to pursue, such as his screen version of the Broadway musical *Jersey Boys* (2014), about the popular singing group the Four Seasons.

However, it is the Clint Eastwood westerns that inform the veteran filmmaker's work in all genres, and that continue to be the strongest reason for his iconic status as both an actor and director.

Note

1. However, if adjusted for inflation, *Every Which Way but Loose* (1978) remains his most financially successful film.

Bibliography

Books

Eliot, Marc. *American Rebel: The Life of Clint Eastwood.* New York: Harmony, 2009.

Frank, Alan. *Clint Eastwood: Screen Greats.* New York: Exeter, 1982.

Frayling, Christopher. *Clint Eastwood.* London: Virgin, 1992.

———. *Sergio Leone: Something to Do with Death.* London: Thames & Hudson, 2005.

Gallafent, Edward. *Clint Eastwood: Actor and Director.* London: Cassell Illustrated, 1994.

———. *Clint Eastwood: Filmmaker and Star.* New York: Continuum, 1994.

Hughes, Howard. *Aim for the Heart: The Films of Clint Eastwood.* London: I. B. Tauris, 2009.

Kapsis, Robert E., and Kathie Coblentz, eds. *Clint Eastwood: Interviews.* Jackson: University Press of Mississippi, 1999.

MacLaine, Shirley. *My Lucky Stars: A Hollywood Memoir.* New York: Random House, 1995.

McGilligan, Patrick. *Clint: The Life and Legend.* London: HarperCollins, 1999.

Munn, Michael. *Clint Eastwood: Hollywood's Loner.* London: Robson, 1992.

O'Brien, Daniel. *Clint Eastwood: Film-Maker.* London: B. T. Batsford, 1996.

Schickel, Richard. *Clint Eastwood: A Biography.* New York: Knopf, 1996.

Siegel, Don. *A Siegel Film: An Autobiography.* London: Faber & Faber, 1993.

Zmijewsky, Boris, and Lee Pfeiffer. *The Films of Clint Eastwood.* Secaucus, NJ: Citadel, 1982.

Magazines, Periodicals, and Monographs

American Film Institute. "Eastwood: In His Own Words." Special Booklet, 1995.

Byskind, Peter. "Any Which Way He Can." *Premiere,* April 1993.

Castos, Gregory. "Eli Wallach Interview." *Filmfax,* February/March 1991.

Chapman, Stephen. "Who Is the Pale Rider?" *Chicago Tribune*, July 7, 1985.

Denby, David. "Clint Eastwood: Immortality in His Sights." *Telegraph*, May 28, 2010.

Ebert, Roger. "Writing the Book on Clint Eastwood." *Chicago Sun Times*, December 7, 1986.

Hicks, Christopher. "Eastwood Remembers 'Fistful of Dollars' Director." *Deseret News*, January 25, 1990.

McGee, Scott. "The Outlaw Josey Wales." Turner Classic Movies. http://www.tcm.com/this-month/article/79824%7C0/The-Outlaw-Josey-Wales.html.

Sachs, Ben. "Exploring the Obsessive Nature of Don Siegel and Clint Eastwood's *The Beguiled*." *Chicago Reader*, November 27, 2012. http://www.chicagoreader.com/Bleader/archives/2012/11/27/exploring-the-obsessive-nature-of-don-siegel-and-clint-eastwoods-the-beguiled.

Smith, Jeff. "Basically, Just a Really Nice Little Girl: Pamelyn Ferdin: Her Life & Work." *Feminist Baseball*, March 1995.

Vincour, John. "Clint Eastwood Seriously." *New York Times*, February 24, 1985.

Wise, Damon. "Clint Eastwood: How the West Was Won." *Empire*, June 1990.

Reviews

Adler, Renata. "Good Bad Ugly." *New York Times,* January 25, 1968.

Byrne, Bridget. "High Plains Drifter." *Los Angeles Herald Examiner*, April 6, 1973.

Canby, Vincent. "Clint Eastwood Is Star of Siegel's 'The Beguiled.'" *New York Times*, April 1, 1971.

———."Coogan's Bluff: Sheriff Eastwood Tangles with the Big City." *New York Times*, October 3, 1968.

———."Heaven's Gate." *New York Times*, November 19, 1980.

———. "'High Plains Drifter' Opens on Screen." *New York Times*, April 20, 1973.

———. "Review/Film: *Unforgiven*: A Western without Good Guys." *New York Times*, August 7, 1992.

———. "Screen: Sheriff Eastwood Tangles with the Big City." *New York Times*, October 3, 1968.

Champlin, Charles. "The Good the Bad and the Ugly." *Los Angeles Times*, January 26, 1968

Crowther, Bosley. "Screen: 'A Fistful of Dollars' Opens: Western Film Clichés All Used in Movie Cowboy Star from TV Featured as Killer." *New York Times*, February 2, 1967.

———. "Screen: 'For Few Dollars More' Opens: Trans-Lux West Shows New Eastwood Film 2 Rivals in Murder Are Presented as Heroes." *New York Times*, July 4, 1967.

———. "For a Few Dollars More." *Chicago Sun Times*, May 15, 1967.

———. "Hang 'Em High." *Chicago Sun Times*, August 5, 1968.

———. "Joe Kidd." *Chicago Sun Times*, July 18, 1972.

———. "The Outlaw Josey Wales." *Chicago Sun Times*, July 1, 1976.

———. "Paint Your Wagon." *Chicago Sun Times*, October 31, 1969.

———. "Pale Rider." *Chicago Sun Times*, June 28, 1985.

———. "Two Mules for Sister Sara." *Chicago Sun Times*, July 1, 1970.

Champlin, Charles. "The Good the Bad and the Ugly." *Los Angeles Times*, January 26, 1968

Ebert, Roger. "City Heat." *Chicago Sun Times*, December 7, 1984.

———. "Heaven's Gate." *Chicago Sun Times,* November 24, 1980.

French, Philip. "Under Western Disguise." *Observer*, June 11, 1967.

Greenspun, Roger. "Joe Kidd (1972). Film: Eastwood Western." *New York Times*, July 20, 1972.

———. "Screen: 'Two Mules for Sister Sara.'" *New York Times*, June 25, 1970.

Kehr, Dave. "The Beguiled." *Chicago Reader*. http://www.chicagoreader.com/chicago/the-beguiled/Film?oid=1063398.

———. "Hang 'Em High." *Chicago Reader*. http://www.chicagoreader.com.

———. "The Outlaw Josey Wales." *Chicago Reader*. http://www.chicagoreader.com/chicago/the-outlaw-josey-wales/Film?oid=2686750.

———. "Sudden Impact." *Chicago Reader*. http://www.chicagoreader.com.

Maslin, Janet. "Eastwood Stars and Directs 'Bronco Billy.'" *New York Times*, June 11, 1980.

People. "People Picks and Pans: 'Firefox,'" July 26, 1982.

Rich, Frank. "Escape from Alcatraz." *Time*, July 2, 1979.

Variety. "The Good the Bad and the Ugly," December 31, 1967.

Websites

Chicago Reader. http://www.chicagoreader.com.

Clint Eastwood Forums. http://www.clinteastwood.org/forums/.

Internet Movie Database. http://www.imdb.com.

Roger Ebert: Great Movies. http://www.rogerebert.com/great-movies.

The Spaghetti Western Database. http://www.spaghetti-western.net.

Wikipedia. http://en.wikipedia.org.

Interviews

Ferdin, Pamelyn. E-mail message to author, June 30, 2014.

Locke, Tammy. Private online message to author, April 4, 2014.

Post, Ted. Telephone interview by author, May 10, 2013.

Spiegel, Scott. E-mail message to author, May 25, 2014.

Index

About the Author

James L. Neibaur is a film historian and retired educator who has written hundreds of articles, including over forty essays for the *Encyclopedia Britannica*. He is also the author of several books on film, including *The Fall of Buster Keaton: His Films for MGM, Educational Pictures, and Columbia* (2010); *Early Charlie Chaplin: The Artist as Apprentice at Keystone Studios* (2011); *The Silent Films of Harry Langdon: 1923–1928* (2012); *The Charley Chase Talkies: 1929–1940* (2013); *The Elvis Movies* (2014); and *James Cagney Films of the 1930s* (2014). With Terri Niemi, Neibaur coauthored *Buster Keaton's Silent Shorts: 1920–1923* (2013).